HOW

THE NIGERIAN ECONOMY

CAN OVERTAKE

THE AMERICAN ECONOMY

SUNDAY ADELAJA

Sunday Adelaja
**HOW THE NIGERIAN ECONOMY CAN OVERTAKE
THE AMERICAN ECONOMY**
©2017 Sunday Adelaja
ISBN 978-1-908040-86-2

Cover design by Alexander Bondaruk
Interior design by Olena Kotelnykova

TABLE OF CONTENTS

INTRODUCTION

I can just imagine what must be running through the minds of those who are reading this extremely catchy title. I can almost envisage some remarks like 'Pastor Sunday has come again', while others will be thinking, *"what a fantasy if not fallacy."*

I don't claim to hold the key of knowledge, I do however, as a student of current affairs, wish to argue my case. I hope my efforts would give hope to Nigerians and Africans everywhere. It is also my hope that the newly elected Nigerian government will hear the voice of reason, study my hypothesis and work hard to actualize them.

Let me start by saying that the key to Nigeria's economy overtaking America's economy, is in CURBING CORRUPTION. I will examine this hypothesis more closely in this book.

CORRUPTION IS AFRICA'S GREATEST PROBLEM. NOT POVERTY. NOT LACK OF RICHES. NOT RACISM.

DENNIS PRAGER

Corruption, that monster that has crippled nations, economies and peoples is our biggest shame and inhibition. If Nigeria could successfully fight corruption on all levels with all our natural and human resource endowments, Nigeria's economy is poised to overtake America's economy in the near future.

To start with, we are going to be looking at corruption in terms of Political Corruption which is the use of power by government officials for illegitimate private gain. An illegal act by an officeholder constitutes political corruption when the act is directly related to their official duties. It is mainly done under guise of law and involves trading in influence.

I don't think I need to waste your precious time my dear readers to try to convince you that our beloved nation Nigeria has broad based corruption. All through the length and breadth of our country, we see corruption everywhere. In the government offices, police check-points, schools, universities, military, Nollywood, media, entertainment industry etc. Friends, no doubt about it, it's either we exterminate corruption or it annihilates us as a nation.

Nigeria, a country richly endowed with natural resources and high quality human capital is yet to find its rightful place among the comity of nations. A major reason that has been responsible for her socio-economic stagnation is the phenomenon of corruption. The central theme of this book rests in the fact that the reason for economic stagnation in the country is largely due to corruption. It is against this background that we explored the corrupt tendencies of the political leadership in Nigeria since 1960 and its implication for socio-economic underdevelopment.

Since independence, Nigeria has been bedeviled by myriads of challenges ranging from ethnicity, bad leadership, economic abyss manifesting in- high rate of youth unemployment, soaring rate of inflation, increased criminal activities, terrorism and breakdown in social values. Of all these challenges, none appears to have tormented Nigeria and Nigerians the most than the pervasive nature of corruption. This has led many people, scholars and laymen alike, to at different times, devote considerable studies to the understanding and explanations of, perhaps, Nigeria's biggest socio-political problem. The problem of political corruption has taken different dimensions at various times and at varying degrees.

It is on this note that the writer argues that but for the seeming ubiquitous nature of corruption in the country, the Nigerian economy has all the potentials to overtake the United States economy. Nigeria has the resources, human and materials, to achieve the "impossible" dream of overtaking the United States as the largest economy in the world. But, first, the country must disinfect itself of the manifest nature of political corruption that has bedeviled it for years. If not, rather than fly with the eagles, the country will continue with the ducks at the lower echelons of the world.

The question had always been whether Nigeria can ever come to the same level with the United States of America (USA), which is the strongest economy in the world. There have been articles, books and in some cases conferences organized for this express purpose.

About $20-trillion had been stolen from Nigeria's coffers by leaders who had access to the nation's money between 1960 and 2005. This was disclosed by Dapo Olorunyomi, chief of staff to the chairman of the Economic and Financial Crimes Commission (EFCC) at a function in Lagos. Olorunyomi, who was speaking at the yearly Dinner/Re-union of the Lagos State chapter of the University of Ilorin Alumni Association, said the figure was sourced from the records of the United Nations Development Programme (UNDP). (Reference:http://nigeriavillagesquare.com/forum/threads/efcc-says-nigerian-leaders-stole-20-trillion-in-45-years.5322/. This report was confirmed by a leading Nigerian newspaper The Vanguard from their publication on March 25th 20015. (Reference: http://www.vanguardngr.com/2015/03/20trn-stolen-from-from-nigerias-treasury-by-leaders-efcc/)

Please pay attention to the above statement once again and I will like you to read it over and over again. Because of how incredible this might sound, I have endeavored to provide the link and to confirm the sources of the information. Please note that the Nigerian Economic and Financial Crimes Commission is probably the most reputed and most credible institution in Nigeria. But besides that they don't want us to just believe their report, even they are referring us to a more reputable international organization in the United Nations Development Programme (UNDP). The reason this is important is because our international readers might find it difficult to believe that such an amount as much as $20 trillion dollars could even be generated in Nigeria to start with, talk less of so much been stolen. To an average Nigerian however, this is not news. They won't find it outrageous to believe that Nigeria is that rich. In fact most Nigerians know that their leaders have stolen more than $20 trillion from the country's coffers.

Oxfam an international confederation of 20 NGOs working with partners in over 90 countries to end the injustices that cause poverty is another source that has confirmed the report from the Economic and Financial Crimes Commission (EFCC) and the United Nations Development Program (UNDP). In the words of their representative, Mr Celestine Odo, of Good Governance Program Coordinator for Oxfam, said that according to the report, public office holders stole an estimated $20 trillion from the treasury between 1960 and 2005, while multinational companies receive tax incentives estimated at $2.9bn a year.

Now what is $20 trillion USD? I have decided to illustrate it to you below so that it can be easily fathomed and believed.

Talking about $20 trillion USD, remember that the Nigerian economy is presently worth only $510 billion USD. For your information the whole European Union is worth only between 17- 20 trillion USD. That is talking about all the 28 countries that are part of the European Union. America which is the single richest country in the world is worth 16-17 trillion USD by GDP as of 2013. At the same time China's GDP was worth 10 trillion USD and Japan 4-5 trillion USD.

Now my friends, I'm sure you can see where I deduced my argument from, that Nigeria's economy can still outgrow America's economy. If the total worth of the American economy today is 16-17 trillion USD by the GDP 2013 and the amount of money stolen from Nigeria in the past 50 years is $20 trillion USD. It means that

Nigeria and Africa in general is indeed a wealthy continent that could become the future economic giant of the world, if we could only get it right. The first thing we must get right is declaring war against corruption. From there, we can begin to put our resources into building a modern and civilized nation and continent. Note that the $20 trillion USD that has been stolen is talking about all the money stolen from all other economic sectors not just oil (including agriculture, finance, natural resources etc.). It is also important to note that this is within the first 45 years of Nigeria's independence. Nigeria is indeed a blessed nation. We are potentially wealthy in all aspects of life. But to preserve and actualize this wealth we all must join the anti-corruption brigade. More so, we all must hate corruption with a passion. We should all support the new government anyway possible to make sure that their campaign promises to fight corruption is fulfilled.

FIGHTING CORRUPTION IS NOT JUST GOOD GOVERNANCE. IT'S SELF-DEFENSE. IT'S PATRIOTISM.

JOE BIDEN

Nigerians never cease to ask, for example, why it is that, at independence in 1960, Nigeria's gross domestic product (GDP) per capita was higher at $559 than that of Singapore's at $476, but today Singapore's GDP per capita, according to World Bank Report in 2016, has grown to $55,182 and Nigeria's has increased to just $3,005? Singapore's per capita GDP is now higher than that of the United States of America. If this had been suggested 50 years ago, that Singapore was going to have a higher per capita GDP than America, most experts would have disputed it, just as they are disputing my argument today that Nigeria's economy can overtake that of the United States.

The question we should honestly ask ourselves as Nigerians therefore is: What is Singapore doing that we are not? If we ask ourselves this hard question, the answer will soon show up. Singapore does not have oil. It does not have as much population as we have. It is below us in resources, both human and mineral. Yet it is economically far ahead of Nigeria today.

Our frank and only answer to this puzzle is corruption. Countries like Singapore chose to fight corruption head on, while we did not!

In a shocking data provided by the former Coordinating Minister and the Minister of finance of the federal government of Nigeria Ngozi Okonjo-Iweala during her address to the Nigerian House of Representatives' Joint Committee on Appropriation/Finance in Abuja in 2013 said, *"We are losing revenue; 400,000 barrels of crude oil are lost on a daily basis due to illegal bunkering, vandalism and production shut-in."*

In one of the greatest news in African continent in the last decade, is the discovery of oil in Ghana. With this discovery, much appears to have been added to the Ghanaian economy that it catapulted Ghana's economy into one of the fastest growing in the world. It is believed that Ghana currently produces about 400,000 barrels of oil per day, which is equal to 400 million USD per day, based on the 2014 price of $100 per barrel.

This news notwithstanding, the amount of oil produced in Ghana is just approximately (creating many

opportunities and bringing joy to the lives and families of millions of Ghanaians and the same amount of
money that has hugely enhanced the economy of Ghana)
is, sadly, the very same amount of crude oil value unaccounted for daily in Nigeria today!

Many have remained stubbornly pessimistic about the
ability of the Nigerian economy to ever be at par with the
US let alone, overtake it. Others have maintained their
hopes that in spite of the present economic challenges,
Nigeria can actually do wonders if the leaders are serious
about it.

The most important thing the Nigerian government
and indeed the Nigerian populace has to be serious
about is in fighting corruption. This has to become a
comprehensive national movement. From the statistics
I have presented above it is easy to see that the Nigerian
economy has the potential not just to overtake the European economy or the Japanese economy, we still stand
a good chance of outgrowing even the largest economy
in the world, the United States of America. Please think
about it: the total amount of money that has been stolen
from Nigeria is $20trillion which is slightly larger than
the current GDP of the United States. Now let us imagine
that Nigeria had not been a corrupt nation and the
$20trillion had not been stolen, we would have repeated
the same feat as Singapore. Singapore overtook America
in per capita economy and Nigeria would have done the
same in the Gross Domestic Product.

It took America 200 years to build such an economy
but with the blessings God has bestowed on Nigeria both
in human and natural resources, it would have taken
Nigeria just over 50 years to build the same economy as

America. This is still not impossible going by the example of China that has become the second largest economy in the world in less than 50 years.

In this book we will try to explore how Nigeria could still make this happen by confronting our biggest nemesis, the giant of corruption.

For the Love of God, Church and Nation
Dr. Sunday Adelaja.

CHAPTER ONE

The Nigerian Economy Can Overtake America's Economy: Fallacy Or Fantasy?

IF THE AMOUNT OF MONEY STOLEN FROM NIGERIA IN THE LAST 30 YEARS WAS STOLEN FROM THE UK, THE UK WOULD CEASE TO EXIST.

DAVID CAMERON, EX-BRITISH PRIME MINISTER

Before we go further, let us come out clear, I don't lay claims to absolute knowledge in the field of economics. The information presented herein, are simply a product of acute observations on the Nigerian affairs since the 1980s. And, as a student of current affairs and developments in the Nigerian society, I present my case as logically as I possibly can. While I understand that the position I will be canvassing are highly debatable, it is our considered opinion that this will widen the scope of public discourse on the potentials of the Nigerian economy to overtake the America's based on the conditions we will be presenting in this book. Surprisingly, these conditions are simple. But, as the Prussian strategist Carl von Clausewitz once wrote in his classic, On War, *"Everything in war is very simple, but the simplest thing is difficult."*

While we are not in doubt that this looks too ambitious or a pipe dream given the present reality, we insist it is possible and achievable. Other nations of the world, like Singapore and China have done the "impossible" why can't Nigeria do the same?

The story is told of a large container so big that a whole village can drink water from it. This container supplies water to the villagers even in draught. The villagers will never need to worry about water during the dry season. Since the villagers' water supply is secure, the neighboring villages began to live, understandably, in envy.

Once, the village king had requested his rival neighboring kings to pay homage to him and this village in exchange for water supply in dry season to their villages. This is something the neighboring villages consider an insult. What could they have done since their God appears not to be fair to them by providing them such a massive container in their villages?

This village grew in prosperity as their farms are almost ever green due to frequent water supply. They enjoyed all these goodies as long as they continued to have water supply.

The other villages which do not possess such natural endowment became so jealous. Some of them soon found a way around it. One of the rival kings then thought he had the solution to the challenge. In alliance with other rival kings, they came up with a plan. The plan was to use some of the villagers to make some inconspicuous holes in the container in such a way that it will be difficult for it to hold water without supplying other villages or wasting. The plan worked because they paid some of the villagers to do the dirty job for them.

The holes went undetected for years, and other confederate villages benefitted from water supply in dry seasons, thanks to the holes which supply water from the large container in the village in our story.

Before long, as a result of expansion and population increase, this once prosperous village began struggling to feed its teeming population. Plants do not grow at their appropriate seasons any longer. The village that supplies neighboring villages' food now is in the middle of famine. As a result of these, fierce struggle over the left over water in the container ensued. Small disagreements soon easily turned to physical battles, in some cases armed conflicts between hitherto friendly families and clans. All these because of shortage of water!

Friends, the story of this village has a lot of similarities with the present situation in our country, Nigeria. Nigeria is a country so blessed by God that other nations are envious of it. It is so blessed that it ordinarily should be the pride of the black man. The only reason it is still lagging behind is continuous leakages taking place in the economy.

Like the village in the story above, Nigerian resources are wasting away either due to continuous wastages manifesting in oil spillages, pipeline bunkering and oil thefts or what some people call capital flights wherein resources that were supposed to be meant for development find their ways into private foreign bank accounts.

Going by the leakages that has taken place in the Nigerian economy without corresponding injections, the results have been discomforting. Like the container in the introductory story, the amount of water leakages without corresponding rainfall leaves the container almost perpetually dry. The problem is not much about Nigerian monies finding their ways into private pockets that those that are lying idle doing absolutely nothing, in foreign bank accounts!

Please take a look at this facts again as was mentioned above:

The question had always been whether Nigeria can ever come to the same level with the United States of America (USA), which is the strongest economy in the world. There have been articles, books and in some cases conferences organized for this express purpose.

About $20-trillion had been stolen from Nigeria's coffers by leaders who had access to the nation's money between 1960 and 2005. This was disclosed by Dapo Olorunyomi, chief of staff to the chairman of the Economic and Financial Crimes Commission (EFCC) at a function in Lagos. Olorunyomi, who was speaking at the yearly Dinner/Re-union of the Lagos State chapter of the University of Ilorin Alumni Association, said the figure was sourced from the records of the United Nations Development Programme (UNDP). (Reference:http://nigeriavillagesquare.com/forum/threads/efcc-says-nigerian-leaders-stole-20-trillion-in-45-years.5322/. This report was confirmed by a leading Nigerian newspaper The Vanguard from their publication on March 25th 20015. (Reference: http://www.

vanguardngr.com/2015/03/20trn-stolen-from-from-ni-gerias-treasury-by-leaders-efcc/)

Please pay attention to the above statement once again and I will like you to read it over and over again. Because of how incredible this might sound, I have endeavored to provide the link and to confirm the sources of the information. Please note that the Nigerian Economic Financial Crimes Commission is probably the most reputed and most credible institution in Nigeria. But besides that they don't want us to just believe their report, even they are referring us to a more reputable international organization in the United Nations Development Program (UNDP). The reason this is important is because our international readers might find it difficult to believe that such an amount as much as $20 trillion dollars could even be generated in Nigeria to start with, talk less of so much been stolen. To an average Nigerian however, this is not news. They won't find it outrageous to believe that Nigeria is that rich. In fact most Nigerians know that their leaders have stolen more than $20 trillion from the country's coffers.

Oxfam an international confederation of 20 NGOs working with partners in over 90 countries to end the injustices that causes poverty is another source that has confirmed the report from the Economic Financial Crimes Commission (EFCC) and the United Nations Development Program (UNDP). In the words of their representative, Mr Celestine Odo, of Good Governance Program Coordinator for Oxfam, said that according to the report, public office holders stole an estimated $20 trillion from the treasury between 1960 and 2005, while multinational companies receive tax incentives estimated at $2.9 bn a year.

Now what is $20 trillion USD? I have decided to illustrate it to you below so that it can be easily fathomed and believed.

Talking about $20 trillion USD, remember that the Nigerian economy is presently worth only $510 billion USD. For your information the whole European Union is worth only between 17- 20 trillion USD. That is talking about all the 28 countries that are part of the European Union. America which is the single richest country in the world is worth 16-17 trillion USD by GDP as of 2013. At the same time China's GDP was worth 10 trillion USD and Japan 4-5 trillion USD.

Now my friends, I'm sure you can see where I deduced my argument from, that Nigeria's economy can still outgrow America's economy. If the total worth of the American economy today is 16-17 trillion USD by the GDP 2013 and the amount of money stolen from Nigeria in the past 50 years is $20 trillion USD. It means that Nigeria and Africa in general is indeed a wealthy continent that could become the future economic giant of the world, if we could only get it right. The first thing we must get right is declaring war against corruption. From there, we can begin to put our resources into building a modern and civilized nation and continent. Note that the $20 trillion USD that has been stolen is talking about all the money stolen from all other economic sectors not just oil (including agriculture, finance, natural resources etc.). It is also important to note that this is within the first 45 years of Nigeria's independence. Nigeria is indeed a blessed nation. We are potentially wealthy in all aspects of life. But to preserve and actualize this wealth we all must join the anti-corruption brigade. More so, we all must hate corruption with a passion. We should all support the new government anyway possible to make sure that their campaign promises to fight corruption is fulfilled.

> FIGHTING CORRUPTION IS NOT JUST GOOD GOVERNANCE. IT'S SELF-DEFENSE. IT'S PATRIOTISM.
>
> JOE BIDEN

DAVID CAMERON ON STOLEN MONEY

Sometime in 2016 in an event to mark Queen Elizabeth's birthday, British Prime Minister, David Cameron, made a passing comment that Nigeria and Afghanistan were *"two of the most fantastically corrupt countries in the world."* The two countries were slated to attend the anti-corruption summit to mark the Queen's birthday.

The news, understandably, sparked public anger in Nigeria. Many felt the statement credited to the British leader was less than fair on the country. Others felt it was a major indictment on a country engaging in a war against corruption led by President Muhammadu Buhari.

To make matters more complicated, President Buhari, who attended the conference on behalf of Nigeria, accepted the allegation. He admitted, in fact, that Nigeria is corrupt and that there was no need for the Prime Minister to apologize since he is not guilty of what he accused us of. All he needed the Prime Minister to do was return all Nigeria's stolen assets in British possession!

This is not to say that countries in Europe and America are not corrupt. Far from it. In fact, Elizabeth Drew in her book, The Corruption of American Politics, called corruption the "money culture" which she argues is not tied to any particular culture but cuts across cultures. She argues: *"Indisputably, the greatest change in Washington over the twenty-five years in its culture, in the way it does its business, and the ever-burgeoning amount of business transactions that go on here has been the pre-occupation with money"*. According to her, money subverts values.

I have gone to the extent of saying this in order to dispel the myth that corruption is inherently Nigerian or African. The only difference between them and African countries is that their monies never leave the borders of their countries. The stolen monies are looted and invested in their countries. *"If the amount of money stolen from Nigeria in the last 30 years was stolen from the UK,"* Cameron was once quoted to have said *"the UK would cease to exist."* This statement is true. A very recent development in Nigeria confirms this. We shall be discussing this in the next section of this chapter.

GOLD IN THE CLAY

Long time ago, I witnessed an auto accident on a Nigerian road. The emergency response was poor. The victims lie there almost lifeless and blood gushing out like water running out of a tap. There seems to be nothing anyone could do, than wait for the ambulance service to respond to distress calls and somehow save the lives of these people.

Help was slow, but finally it came. I watched the doctors treat the victims who were desperately in need of blood. They have lost so much blood due to different degrees of injuries in different parts of their bodies. One of the victims needed blood urgently, but the blood in the hospital bank did not match his blood type. We had to rush to get the samples that match the victims, else he dies. Some of us rushed to different hospitals we knew, hoping to get the right blood type. We got the blood in the end, and maybe, that saved the victim's life.

The other patient, lost blood, like the first, but not as much. Her own case has little to do with loss of blood but from some complications due to clotting of blood. This, according to the doctors, was more dangerous than loss of blood. The blood has no use in the body if it cannot circulate.

This story again shows the Nigerian present situation. First, the country's resources find their way into foreign accounts through leakages arising from theft and looting. Second, the monies buried in holes and abandoned properties cause more damages that those that are taken outside the country.

Friends, please do not get me wrong. Both situations pose serious negative implications for the country's economy. The comparison between them is only relative.

Recently, one of the most mind blowing of discoveries by the Buhari administration was the news of the USD$9.8 million and another 75,000 British pounds which was connected to the former group managing director of the Nigerian National Petroleum Corporation (NNPC) Mr. Andrew Yakubu was recovered after a raid was carried out at one of his houses in Kaduna State. The money was hidden in such a way that it could not be discovered by someone who did not have prior knowledge. The perpetrators allegedly had gone to the extent of even providing a fire proof protection for the safe.

Though, Mr. Yakubu, will later claim the money was a gift, but the implications of hiding such money in an unoccupied building makes the whole matter suspicious.

To make matters worse, a few days later, the Economic and Financial Crimes Commission (EFCC), Nigeria's anti-corruption agency, again, recorded another ground breaking discovery, when they found a house in Banana Island, Lagos, which is worth a whopping USD $37.5 million.

Let us simplify these figures so that some of our lay readers can understand them. At the foreign exchange rate of N300 per dollar and N500 per pound, $9.8 million will give us N2.94 billion; 75,000 British pounds will give us N37.5 million and $37.5 million gives us N11.3 billion. Adding these figures together, we have approximately N14.3 billion which is a significant fraction of the national budget and a little lower than some states' budget for education annually!

We all know that gold is found in clay. But to get its true value, it must be extracted, refined and transformed. The gold in clay ordinarily has no value until it is unearthed.

For the Nigerian economy to overtake the US, all our stolen resources hidden in foreign banks and in abandoned buildings must be unearthed. They must be returned to the government's coffers. They must be put into productive uses like investment in education and health that our citizens will benefit from.

The money found in places like Yakubu's hometown in Southern Kaduna must be recovered by any means necessary. These are the resources we need to develop our economy. We cannot continue to go cap in hand begging for foreign investors to come into our economy when we all have the resources required to develop our economy into a First World economy.

Unfortunately, these resources are hidden in holes in private inaccessible houses. Some are in the forests for fear of being detected.

Like the ex-British Prime Minister, Cameron, has said, monies like these cannot be taken out of an economy and it still remains healthy. Just like the accident victim that needs blood to survive as said above, it needs the monies back. Unlike the victim who needs the blood of other people to survive, ours need its resources that were stolen from it in the first place.

We think that President Buhari said the right thing when he boldly and confidently told Mr. Cameron that Nigeria and Nigerians do not need apologies, she needs back her stolen assets hidden in European and American banks!

HOW NIGERIA'S ECONOMY CAN OVERTAKE AMERICA'S ECONOMY

I can just imagine what must be running through the minds of those who are reading this extremely catchy title, How the Nigerian Economy Can Overtake America's Economy. Some will simply dispense it with the wave of the hand or, worse still, will just move over the book at the bookstore. You must be really interested in the development of Nigeria for you to have come this far in reading this book.

"How can Nigeria's economy overtake America's economy?" Is a question that can look spectacular to some Nigerians. The question may also be a hypothesis when rephrased, **"Can Nigeria's economy overtake America's economy?"** Some others may even take the question with a scolding frown. All these reactions are understandable. We intend, in this book, to provide answers, to those who may question this statement.

The key to Nigeria's economy overtaking America's economy, is in CURBING CORRUPTION.

At this point, let us agree with Dennis Prager when he wrote:

> CORRUPTION IS AFRICA'S GREATEST PROBLEM. NOT POVERTY. NOT LACK OF RICHES. NOT RACISM.
>
> DENNIS PRAGER

Let us substitute "Nigeria" for "Africa" and "tribalism" for "racism" in Mr. Prager's verdict. What we have is that "Corruption is Nigeria's greatest problem. Not poverty. Not lack of riches. Not tribalism."

The challenges we have faced over the years is that people saw the problem(s) of Nigeria as poverty, tribalism or ethnic conflict. In some cases, lack of resources. The people who adopt this perspective do not seem to understand the fact that poverty, lack of resources, ethnicity conflict and tribalism are simply manifestations of the problem of corruption. We will need to prove this statement with some verifiable facts.

Let us start with the case of Chief James Ibori which is more recent. On 17 April, 2012, former governor of Delta state, James Ibori, was sentenced to 13 years in prison by a Royal Court in London after pleading guilty to charges of money laundering and corruption. The story of the drama surrounding his arrest and repatriation to London from Dubai is too well-known and should not take much of our time here. Why was Ibori found guilty of corruption in London for offences some Nigerian Courts have "cleared" him over? This question bothers on corruption especially in the Judiciary which is beyond the present scope of this book. In all, the dramatic ethnicization of the whole Ibori saga shows how corruption in Nigeria has taken ethnic dimension. Let us look at the particulars of his loot!

Ibori reportedly stole US$250 million (N75 billion if we assume USD $1= N300) from the Nigerian public purse, Ibori pleaded guilty to ten counts of money laundering and conspiracy to defraud at Southwark Crown Court, London. The question is, what can N75 billion do to the Nigerian economy?

First, Ibori's N75 billion loot would have improved allocations to federal universities by 100%. Using the 2015 allocations to ten federal universities which is an average of N7.5 billion per year. If we have say, 36 universities with a grant of N2 billion each, we would have increased their grants by over a hundred percent with the injection of additional N12.1 billion leaving us with a balance of N63 million for our polytechnics, colleges of education and technical schools.

With N75 billion looted by Ibori, we can have about ten different world class research centers each costing about N7 billion.

Second, even at an exaggerated cost of N238 million (or $1 million) to construct roads in Nigeria, N75 billion will construct over 300 good roads (mainly feeder roads) that will last over a hundred years (excluding inflated contracts).

Third, Ibori's loot can construct over 3000 primary health centers across the 774 Local Government areas assuming each will cost N25 million each. This is presently above the capital budget for health in the 2016 budget. Injecting this N75 billion can improve our primary health care delivery system in a country where child mortality rate is seriously high. For example, Mercy Hospital in Merced, California, a state-owned medical Centre has 185 beds and cost $166 million when it was built five years ago. At less than $1 million per bed, it was considered quite economical, especially for California. With Ibori's $250 million loot, we can have two state of the art hospitals in Nigeria!

At an abysmal pay of N60,000 as salary monthly, which is just USD$249 monthly or £157 British Pounds monthly, we can increase our defense budget by fivefold with N75 billion and motivate our soldiers and security forces to defeat Boko Haram. I will also use this opportunity to call for improvement of welfare of our servicemen.

It is on record that Oghara people, Ibori's hometown in Delta state, effectively prevented the arrest of Ibori for what they perceived as persecutions of their "illustrious son" in 2007. As though that were not enough, there is a strong position among his ethnic group that he is one of the defenders of resource control, so that should immune him from corruption trial.

On his reported release, politicians from his ethnic group praised Ibori to the heavens, treating him as a hero of some sorts. The Urhobo Progressive Union (UPU) for instance described his arrest and trial as the *"evil activities of those who dread his rise and courage in championing"* their ethnic cause (Vanguard, 23 December, 2016). The UPU leader, Chief Joseph Omene, according to Vanguard speaking for the group said they celebrated Ibori because he *"puts the Urhobo nation on the radar of national illumination and consciousness."*

While men of honor in the society have since condemned these actions, we need to understand some things in this case:

First, in this man's village, there are no good roads; pipe borne water or functional schools. The money this man stole is enough to send all the children, aged 6-15, to school with one meal a day for six years.

In her study, Mary-Ann Nkolikamma Anisiudo conducted in Anambra, found out that the cost of secondary education in the state, which is more populous that Delta, in 2016, is "N141,680.64 (N141.7 million) which covered public, private and mission schools in first, second and third terms of an academic session; the average cost of senior secondary education for private schools is higher than mission schools while public schools have the lowest mean cost; the mean cost of senior secondary education for students in S. S. III is higher than the cost incurred by students in S. S. I while students in S. S. II incurred the lowest cost of senior secondary education..." Though we can dispute this data as frivolous and extremely exaggerated when compared to the level of education in Nigeria, but let us take it as given. If we agree with this data, that a whole state's cost of education is about N142 million, this simply means that, with N75 billion, we can make literacy out of over 500 teenagers and young adults for one year!

Secondly, when this man was released from prison, his people gave him a heroic welcome. A church service was held in his honor. With a mentality like this, one will see why Nigeria is still a Third World country rather than a First world country where it is supposed to belong!

Thirdly, corruption, that monster that has crippled nations, economies and peoples is our biggest shame and inhibition. If Nigeria could successfully fight corruption on all levels with all our natural and human resource endowments, Nigeria's economy is poised to overtake America's economy in the near future.

Another politician that attracted our attention is a former governor of the oil-rich Bayelsa state, late Chief Diepreye Alamieyeseigha. In the case of Alamieyeseigha, the former governor was charged, like his Delta state counterpart, with looting the state treasury. According to the New York Times (October 14, 2015) he was reputed to have looted the sum of $55 million as governor. Unlike Ibori, he was tried in Nigeria, after escaping controversially dressing like a woman from London.

Friends, USD $55 million at the rate of N300 per US dollar, leaves us with N16.5 billion. Even with the fall in the value of the naira, N16.5 billion will construct 10 different standard libraries at N1.6 billion each. Such research centers will be worth the investments. Today, most of our libraries in our public and private universities don't have up to date materials. Investing $55 million to build 10 solid research centers will be a worthwhile investment in the educational sector.

During one of our visit to a hospital, I met a cancer patient. This hitherto beautifully-looking young lady, who should be in her 30s, had begun to look pale, and dying. Her hair loss was obvious. Her body was progressively deteriorating; even the nurses do not appear interested in her. None of the other patients in the ward wanted to look at her eyes because they looked scary.

This lady was not born that way. She was born beautiful, at least as her old pictures reveal. Her body system has been compromised or corrupted by previously undetected cancerous cells. These cancerous cells progressively contaminated other cells in her mammary gland and had led to serious deformities in the organ.

Things will get better, she thought. Rather than they getting better, they turned worse. She started feeling severe; excruciating pains in her left breast one morning she knew she needed to see the doctor. Tests were carried out when the pains will not abate. It was one of these tests that reveal some tumor had developed in her mammary gland. She was referred to an oncologist who warned her of the dangers of living the tumor to grow further. Since she did not have the money to carry out the operation prescribed, she took some of the drugs the doctors prescribed. She never understood the emergency of her situation until after a month she began to notice decays on her breast. That was how she got herself into the hospital.

We have told this story to make us understand the dangers of uncontrolled corruption. Like the tumor or cancerous cells, they are malignant. They can kill not only the economy, but the nation itself. The organism, like the cancer patient in our story, would have lived a better, healthier and more fulfilled life had they controlled the tumors or curbing their growth.

In order for the Nigerian economy to overtake America's economy, we must first see the scourge of corruption as a national emergency that concerns us all and must collectively fight. This then will be the fighting point. Only a healthy body can run let alone, overtake in an athletic race.

In the next chapter, we shall be describing corruption and its dimensions pertaining to how they affect the Nigerian economy. We shall be setting the template of the need to curb the monster, before it kills the economy.

CHAPTER TWO

Introducing The Monster Called Corruption

THE DUTY OF THE YOUTH IS TO CHALLENGE CORRUPTION.

KURT COBAIN

When people describe corruption many do not really know what we are talking about. The problem has always been that many do not really know they are describing a monster.

Because of corruption:

1. We don't have enough universities. As a result, our young men and women are scattered all over the world looking for admissions and spending billions of parental hard earned money in the process.

2. Our teachers and professors cannot be properly paid, leading to incessant strikes, boycotts and closures.

3. Both large and middle scale projects are left uncompleted; buildings, airports, highways, hospitals, stadiums etc. litter the whole country.

4. Millions of children are dying of malnutrition and lack of food.

5. So many families go to bed on empty stomachs.

6. Our maternal and child-mortality rate is one of the highest in the world because of our substandard medical services.

7. Our roads claim thousands of lives each year because of their deplorable state.

8. Investments are kept out of our economy.

9. More than half of the population of Nigeria lives on less than 1USD per day.

10. The actions of militant groups in the Niger delta and even such deadly organization as Boko Haram, Kidnappings etc. are all fueled directly or indirectly by corruption.

An acquaintance of mine was once approached by a young man, a civil servant who said: *"Pastor, what do you expect me to do when what I earn is not even enough to take me till end of the month and I have a family and bills to pay? Should I commit suicide by not collecting bribes?"*

I understood the position of this man intimately. If not for the bribes he collects in his office (which issues licenses) this man will in all honesty be committing suicide. To make ends meet, he has to collect bribes in his office and cutting short the licensing process for those who can pay the price. Is this corruption?

Let me give another illustration. A friend of mine happened to be a regular visitor to a public library back then in Nigeria. One of the library attendants had become a friend. Soon, he started talking to my friend about his personal issues, his family problems and his finances. His take home pay does not really take him home. He is a strong Christian and detests bribes.

Because this man is committed to doing his job to the best of his abilities, some of the library users, who must have noticed his incredible positive attitude, began giving him money and other gifts. With these gifts, this man could begin "enjoying his job".

I cited the two scenarios above to show that the meaning of the word "corruption" appeared to have been lost. There is now a thin line between "gifts" and "bribes". Acts of corruption in some cases seem to be more of "it's our culture" no longer the criminal acts they were meant to be!

It is on this note that we need to clarify our position about what we mean by corruption.

WHAT IS CORRUPTION?

If there is any word that has become so familiar to all Nigerians, including two-year olds, it is the question of corruption. Like cancer, corruption weakens the organs of the body; it stunts growth and inhibits development.

Corruption is fast becoming of critical importance in all political systems, but mainly in developing countries. Unfortunately, although more studies are being published on the issue, it remains an elusive topic. This is partly due to the surreptitiousness of activities associated with it, partly due to its obvious links with many traditional cultural forms, and the tendency by academic writers not to wish to ascribe blame to them. Most prominently perhaps, corruption defies easy treatment because of the complexity of the socioeconomic relationships directly responsible for its presence and reach. Corruption performs tacit functions in all societies. In the Western world, corruption in all its manifestations is now regarded as an evil, an unethical set of activities that hinder economic and social development. Indeed, notwithstanding academic studies that saw corruption as a force that should be understood as intimately linked to primordial and traditional loyalties and that may even have certain limited beneficial functions, there is no gainsaying that eradicating corruption has become a laudable ethical imperative in all societies. Nigeria is no exception.

Although corruption is said to exist semper et ubique, this book focuses on Nigeria primarily because this "garden of Eden," with its abundant wealth in crude oil and natural gas, is one of the most underdeveloped regions in the world, largely from the effects of corruption and directionless leadership. More than half a century of independence, it has been reduced to, according to a Nigerian Professor of Political Science, Eghosa Osaghae in his book, Nigeria Since Independence: Crippled Giant, "crippled giant" - a crumbling edifice, built on the rickety foundations of oil rents collected and squandered by its greedy leaders. In spite of its enormous oil wealth, a Nigerian scholar, Jerome Afeikhena drawing upon a World Bank report, estimates that "about 80 percent of Nigeria's oil and natural gas revenues accrue to one percent of the country's population. The other 99 percent of the population receive the remaining 20 percent of the oil and gas revenues, leaving Nigeria with the lowest per capita oil export earning put at $212 per person in 2004". Worse still, most of the wealth that accrues to the 1 percent of the Nigerians - the elites - who have ransacked the "national oil cake" ends up outside the country: "Nigeria had an estimated $107 billion of its private wealth held abroad". As a result, most Nigerians are excluded from the benefits of the oil wealth, and most of the wealth has not been invested within the country, helping to keep most Nigerians below the poverty line.

This book expounds the thesis that corruption is negatively correlated to economic growth and development. In particular, it argues that corrupt and inept leadership is responsible for the state of underdevelopment bedeviling the Nigerian economy. As Nigerian foremost novelist, Chinua Achebe puts it in his An Image of Africa: *"The trouble with Nigeria is simply and squarely a failure of leadership"* (p. 22). The Commission for Africa in its report, titled Our Common Interest published in 2005 has been even more emphatic in excoriating Nigeria's leaders for their lack of a sense of 'noblesse oblige': Nigeria *"has suffered from [leaders] that have looted the resources of the state; that could not or would not deliver services to their people; that in many cases were predatory, corruptly extracting their country's resources; that maintained control through violence and bribery; and that squandered and stole aid"* (p. 106).

I however personally think that the Nigerian leadership problem is overrated. It is my belief that the corruption of the Nigerian populace is a bigger problem than that of the leadership. I have addressed this problem and topic in my book titled, Nigeria and the Leadership Question.

To start with, we are going to be looking at corruption in terms of political corruption which is the use of power by government officials for illegitimate private gains. An illegal act by an officeholder constitutes political corruption when the act is directly related to their official duties. It is mainly done under guise of law and involves trading in influence.

Corruption is one of the most mentioned words in Nigerian politico-social lexicon, but unfortunately, has too many meanings and interpretations. In an attempt to settle this ambiguity, the Transparency International (TI) defined it as *"the misuse of entrusted power for private benefits"*. According to Transparency, facilitation of payments, where a bribe is paid to receive preferential treatment for something that the bribe receiver is required to do by law comprise the former; the latter, however, is a bribe paid to obtain services the bribe receiver is prohibited from providing. To put as a matter of fact corruption, if we agree with Sadig Rasheed, in his contribution to the African Leadership Forum series, titled: **"Corruption, Ethics, and Accountability in Africa: Toward a Responsive Agenda for Action"** is theft of public resources by civil servants; illegal taxation of economic activity; nepotism, including favoring relatives, friends, and other acquaintances in the distribution of public goods, services, and employment in the public sector; embezzlement of public funds; the misuse of public office to extract extralegal income and other benefits for officeholders; capricious and selective enforcement of government regulations to benefit regulators; and differential treatment of business owners in the expectation of bribes from entrepreneurs being granted preferential treatment.

Given the dangerous dimension the phenomenon of corruption has taken in recent times, it is our humble view that it should be the concern for all rather than the scholars alone. Hence the need for these scholars to involve their readers and listeners in the process of analysis and explanation by making their presuppositions and, therefore, their prejudices and predilections explicit in their works. There seem to be no other way out!

We will start this discussion of corruption in Nigerian society by offering a definition of corruption informed by philosophical and moral presuppositions which other people may find unacceptable. Corruption in our view is a form of anti-social behavior by an individual or social group which confers unjust or fraudulent benefits on its perpetrators, is inconsistent with the established legal norms and prevailing moral ethos of the land and is likely to subvert or diminish the capacity of the legitimate authorities to provide fully for the material and spiritual wellbeing of all members of society in a just and equitable manner. I attempt to list below all the presuppositions that I can explicitly identify as informing the definition stated above and my whole analytical, explanatory and prescriptive approach to the issue of corruption in Nigeria:

1. Corruption was not invented by, nor is it peculiar to Nigerians. On the contrary, it is a global phenomenon with deep historical roots, although

it manifests itself with significant similarities and differences in different societies, depending on the peculiar systems of power distribution and the legal and moral norms operating therein.

2. Corruption, like all social phenomena, is intelligible only in its total social context: its peculiar form, dynamics and degree of social and cultural acceptability or tolerance being critically related to the dominant mode of capital accumulation; income, wealth and poverty distribution; power configuration; and the underpinning moral and ethical values operating in a given society.

3. Corruption in Nigeria is a kind of social virus which is a hybrid of traits of fraudulent anti-social behavior derived from British colonial rule and those derived from, and nurtured in the indigenous Nigerian context.

In his book, Stratagems and Spoils, F.G. Bailey writes about corruption by giving the following graphic explanation of the phenomenon. He writes that from time immemorial, *"...there has existed for many years a category of men who make a profession of bridging the gap between the peasants and the administrative and political elite. For the peasants, these are men who know where to get a license for a short gun, how to get a real injection in the hospital instead of distilled water, how to get the file of a court case moved from the bottom of the list to the top or how to keep the file out of the court's hands until one of the litigants gives up in despair or runs out of money, and a variety of other ways of 'fixing', virtually all of which are normative – very forbidden in the rules of bureaucracy, being considered corrupt. Indeed, money changed hands..."*

Though, the book was published in 1980 and describes the situation then in the United States, the picture painted still describes the reality of our situation in Nigeria today. The concept of political godfathers, which has entrenched in Nigeria's political lexicon depicts this situation. Nigeria has a history of political god fathers like late Alhaji Lamidi Adedibu, Chief Chris Uba, Dr. Olusola Saraki and the likes. All these persons fixed their godsons in positions of power in their different states: Oyo, Anambra, Kwara and the likes on the promises of the latter transferring huge sums of public resources to the former and the godfathers controlling and appointing several political officers in their respective states.

The use of power in unethical ways in order to have an advantage among one's opponents or parties seems to have disturbingly become a normal phenomenon in our society today. This is why "gift" is seen not to be voluntary anymore. This crude use of power is manifested in several forms like the use of money to influence the members of the National Assembly. The open display of the notorious "Ghana Must Go" bags loaded with raw cash are seen in the Legislative chambers during ministerial screenings fuels allegations that money exchanged hands. A former minister of the Federal Capital Territory, Mallam Nasir El-Rufai alleged that some Senators demanded money from him before he could be cleared as minister in 2003. Allegations like this only further weaken the legislature that is supposed to be the champion of the anti-corruption fight.

The erosion of societal values has been enormous and urgently calls for concern. This has become so serious that corruption has led to the debasement of citizens' rights and welfare. Contractors do shabby jobs passed as "roads" since he has paid a substantial part of his mobilization fees as gratifications to some corrupt public officials before the contract agreement was signed.

In several societies, especially in Africa, there is varying acceptance of gift-giving. In Africa, this is often used to cement existing relationships or build bridges. This itself is not bad. Many do not, unfortunately, see bribery as something bad or a form of corruption, because in some African traditions, there are thing lines between giving and bribery. Take for instance the Yoruba proverb: *"Bi omode bamo owo we, a bagba jeun"* which means, *"If the young knows how to grease or wash the palms, he can dine with the elders."*

From what we have seen so far, it is clear that corruption is an act performed by a person whose behavior is considered anti-social or immoral. One way to look at it is that for corruption to take place, at least two persons must be involved, an initiator and a receiver. An initiator is the person who gives the bribe to the receiver who collects the bribe.

There are different methods of corruption and corruption itself manifests in several forms. Some corrupt cases are obvious as in the case of a police officer on duty demanding and collecting bribe from a commercial bus conductor while others are not so obvious. Those that are not so obvious are cases of over-invoicing in the case of procurement contracts and poor construction jobs in public works.

The corrupt and fraudulent accumulation of wealth has resulted, over time, in the progressive and phenomenal syphoning of Nigerian resources by politicians, the emptying of the national treasury and the indebtedness of the country almost to the point of bankruptcy: hence the critical dearth of resources for investment on the social, economic and overall cultural development of the masses of our people. Nigeria is, therefore, in a paradoxical situation in which the scandalous, almost legendary, wealth of key ruling class members exists to mock the unspeakable mass poverty, misery and degradation of the Nigerian people. This has, in turn brought about a situation of potential and actual violent confrontation between the ruling elite minority and the majority paupers and destitute; within which context the current urban phenomenon of 'area boys' is just a minor manifestation. This situation is also highly productive, at the attitudinal level, of mass cynicism about, and distrust of the political elite, and constitutes a major factor in the persistence of inter- and intra-communal disunity, antipathy and strife, as well as the progressively worsening problem of political and social instability since independence. Since the public treasury has been the primary and ultimate source of rapid and sensational private accumulation by the Nigerian political elite, the struggle to capture political power (and, therefore, the national treasury) among factions of the ruling class has become progressively acrimonious and bitter. This is because in this kind of struggle which ends in a winner-take-all resolution, the losing factions tend to be rigorously excluded from sharing in the loot. Hence, the invariable tendency among elite factions to use the poor masses from their areas of origin (village, town, local government, state or ethnic group) as cannon fodder and battering rams against their rivals and competitors from other areas, thus further dividing the people and undermining the stability of the society that is already profoundly unstable.

The obsession of many members of the elite with primitive private accumulation at the expense of the public means that they tend to divert resources earmarked for running and maintaining public institutions in their charge (institutions like hospitals, schools, universities, public utilities, the judiciary, the police and even the armed forces) to corrupt private purposes. By so doing, they subvert these institutions and their capacity to perform their assigned tasks efficiently, thereby damaging the substantive interests and endangering the lives of citizens whom these public institutions are meant to serve. Through the systematic pillage of the nation's wealth by its supposed custodians over several decades, many young Nigerians of lowly origins, after successfully passing out of schools, universities and other institutions of learning, cannot find gainful employment. This is because resources, which could have been used for job creation, have been looted by the leaders. As a consequence many of these educated young people are either 'brain drained' to other lands in search of greener pastures, or get diverted into various criminal ways of making a livelihood like armed robbery, prostitution, drug peddling and trafficking and all manner of racketeering. In this and other ways, greedy Nigerian leaders have squandered the future of their country and its children, and reduced Nigeria to its present status of a pariah in the comity of nations.

TYPOLOGY OF CORRUPTION

I don't think it will be necessary to waste your time to convince you on the prevalence of corruption in Nigeria. You only need to take a walk to our public schools, hospitals, utilities, police, media, military and the likes and you will be convinced that truly, corruption lives in Nigeria.

In his wonderful work, Corruption in Nigeria: A New Paradigm for Effective Control, Victor Dike identifies three typologies of corruption. These are: political or grand corruption, bureaucratic or petty corruption and economic corruption.

ECONOMIC CORRUPTION

When people talk about corruption in Nigeria, little do they know it has multiple dimensions. Economic corruption has a direct damaging effect on the economy than other types of corruption. This includes but not limited to bribery, fraud, embezzlement, extortion, misappropriation and the likes.

According to Dike, in his conception of economic corruption, it includes:

1. Bribery: when someone pays, in cash or in kind, for something taken or given in a relationship both parties have a foreknowledge that is corrupt. A drive from Lagos to Ibadan will scandalize a first time visitor to the country on the number of Police checkpoints. These checkpoints should

ordinarily be a security measure, but these have been turned into points of bribe collection from motorists and in some cases, commuters.

2. Embezzlement is another notorious aspect of economic corruption. This involves the theft of state resources. In this case, a public official simply corners public resources for his own private use(s). The embezzlement of public funds is one of the most common types of corruption in Nigeria.

In Nigeria, there are often very poor regulatory systems in public procurements systems which give room for a wide space for looting the treasury. According to the Economic and Financial Crimes Commission (EFCC) about $20 trillion USD has been stolen from the treasury or embezzled by leaders who had access to the nation's money between 1960 - 2005. We must also note that this is not including the 6 years under the leadership of President Jonathan.

POLITICAL CORRUPTION

Political corruption is often more pronounced than economic corruption because it takes place at the highest level of authority. In Nigeria, in the absence of many indigenous industrialists, political decision makers take the ultimate decisions. It is often difficult and frustrating when, those whose responsibility it is to make laws to curb corruption are themselves corrupt.

Political corruption becomes so dangerous because virtually all institutions in the society are tied to the political institutions. Laws made by politicians affect the

Churches and other religious institutions. So, when this institution become corrupt or corrupted, the Church itself is not safe!

There is the story of a pastor in 2014 whose private jet was involved in an illegal transfer of some huge amounts of money to South Africa. When the authorities in South Africa arrested the jet, there came "religious" dimensions to the news. The jet was arrested because the owner (a Pentecostal pastor) ran out of favor with the Orthodox Church; the Church is being persecuted because it is supporting a Christian candidate in an election; the pastor has been an outspoken supporter of the government and the likes. All these are things you get when the political system is so corrupt.

The Yorubas have a saying that when the fish will decay, it starts from the head. The fish does not start decaying from the tail. So, political corruption is something that should worry us all if we are serious about any serious economic growth in Nigeria.

BUREAUCRATIC CORRUPTION

In this case, we are talking about corruption in the Civil Service. The politicians need the civil servants to sign the files to give some degree of legitimacy to corruption. The civil servant only needs to be given his own token or "carried along" to sign or move the files after money or some other pecuniary benefits have been given.

A walk to a government ministry or corporation today will almost leave one frustrated. A colleague of mine shared his experience while he went to apply for a PhD scholarship in a state's ministry of education.

At the entry, the security man gives him the impression that the environment is for "serious" business. He was directed to the Scholarship Department where he would obtain his form. On getting to the Department, he met a woman who was supposed to attend to him.

"Form don finish" - she said in a rather rude voice.

"But they published it in the newspaper just yesterday." - My friend said.

This young woman laughed loudly and suddenly looked at him and said - *"Who told you Scholarship is for people like you?"*

Dumfounded, my friend said - *"I am a PhD student at the University. So who is the scholarship meant for if I may ask?"*

"You wan know?"

"Yes" - he said

"I can give you the form if you are ready. But for now, you don't look ready."

"Madam you are confusing me. First, you said the forms have finished. Later you said the form was not for people like me. Later you said if I am ready. If I am not ready I would not leave my house to come to this place."

At this point, my friend was doing his best not to lose his temper because that could effectively end all hopes of getting the state scholarship. So, quietly, my friend asked (with a smile) - *"How can I be ready because I need this thing badly?"*

The young woman smiled and said - *"Now you are talking. You will have to Grease palms."*

My friend at this point could no longer pretend not to understand the genesis of the rude woman's initial attitude. It was all for him to "pay" for the scholarship form that was supposed ordinarily to be free of charge, at least the advertorial said!

Let us look at another case. Bola Adebosun left work one evening during his first week on the job as a Food Inspection Officer (FIO), in the Ministry of Health. Soon, he was overheard grumbling, *'I am going to wring the neck of every corrupt official I come across. I am going to salvage the image of this Ministry if it's the last thing I do.'* Bola who recently turned 29, had just been appointed to the powerful position in the state. The Health Ministry had reputation for being one of the most corrupt organizations in the state. Bola, with this understanding, quickly appreciated how lucrative a Health Ministry position could be for one of the youngest nutritionists in the country. Most employees owned cars. A majority possessed bungalows. Some officials were almost legends in their own time:

- Mr. Bashir worked as a Deputy Manager in one of the agencies under the ministry in a small town, near one of the state's ports. In his mid-40s, Basir had been a Deputy Manager for 12 years and had refused two opportunities to be promoted and move from the present position. He was known to enjoy wine and women and was frequently found in the high-rolling Beach Hotel in the city. On one occasion, he was seen walking out of the nightclub after having lost his wallet. 'Oh, it doesn't matter', he said, 'there was only 5000 pounds in it'. Bashir's annual salary from the government was about 6000 pounds.

- Mr. Niyi was a District Food Controller in a coastal town of the state. He was asked to remove about 1000 gunny bags of defective wheat from the Health Ministry's warehouse and destroy them. Instead, he removed the bags of perfectly edible wheat and sold it in the interior of the province for a fabulous sum. The people of the town continued to receive bad wheat. Finally, a citizens' delegation travelled 400 km to the Minister of Food's office in the capital, and protested. The Minister visited the town and saw the defective wheat in the ration shops. Niyi's fate was a transfer to another local government in the state where he was often seen enjoying his shiny new car.

The government had just retrenched a large number of workers due to wide ranges of corruption allegations. Bola's predecessor in the office was himself famous for corruption. He was appointed because he was from the same tribe with the Permanent Secretary in the ministry. He had sometimes used his powers of summary proceedings to threaten or banish employees who were not loyal-incidentally showing higher officials that actions were being taken against 'the corrupt'. This situation was considered a normal phenomenon and was accepted by the employees of the ministry. At least, it was normal when the Permanent secretary was sacked and another was brought to the post.

Bola's story above is the familiar narrative of corruption in the civil service in Nigeria.

While there are just thin lines between Dike's classification of corruption, just two (political and bureaucratic corruption) will bother us in this chapter. This is not to say that other types of corruption, say electoral corruption, are not as deadly or monstrous, but because they are immediately irrelevant to the central theme of this book.

Our conception of corruption refers to illicit acts by a politician or decision-maker who uses his or her position to enrich himself or his immediate or extended family. The manifestations of this includes: fraud, nepotism, bribery, embezzlement, favoritism, misappropriation and in some cases, trickery.

I don't think I need to waste your precious time my dear readers to try to convince you that our beloved nation Nigeria has broad based corruption. All through the length and breadth of our country, we see corruption everywhere. In the government offices, police check-points, schools, universities, military, Nollywood, media, entertainment industry etc. Friends, no doubt about it, it's either we exterminate corruption or it annihilates us as a nation.

CHAPTER THREE

The Political Economy of Wastage in Nigeria

SO WHEN THEY WERE FILLED, HE SAID TO HIS DISCIPLES, GATHER UP THE FRAGMENTS THAT REMAIN, SO THAT NOTHING IS LOST.

JOHN 6:12 (BIBLE)

In this chapter, we shall be taking a look at the opportunity costs of corruption. Remember we are only examining the $200 billion that was lost within the years of 2009 to 2015 from the oil industry. Let's examine some of the benefits that Nigerian economy could have had if this money was left in the coffers of government.

1. The cost of 1000 MW of a gas power electricity plant is 1 billion USD. With $200 billion USD we could produce enough electricity to rival any developed country. For example South Africa produces just over 40MW, UK also. We can produce 4 times that amount, and with electricity, our development would be hugely accelerated.

2. $200 billion USD will provide safe and clean water to the entire world for 20 years. (8 billion people) because the price for providing water for the whole world is 10 billion a year.

3. $200 billion USD can provide MMR vaccine for every child in the world, 20 times over.

4. $200 billion USD will pay for the registration of all aspiring Nigerian youths who want to register for WAEC and UTME at the rate of 25, 000 Naira per student. Let's say Nigerian youths are 70 million in number, it could pay for them for 20 years consecutively.

5. With $200 billion USD we can sponsor the whole United Nations relief operation for 15 years consecutively, bearing in mind that for the year 2014 the budget for relief operation was $13 billion USD.

6. With $200 billion USD we could feed the entire Nigeria population of 170 million people free for 10 months.

7. The biggest banks in Nigeria, for example First Bank or Zenith Bank are priced at $20 billion dollars. We could have 10 more of those banks.

8. With $200 billion USD we could sponsor over 2000 Nigerian's mission to Mars. India spent 75 million dollars on their mission to Mars.

9. With $200 billion USD we could rebuild Nigerian airways and equip it with the latest Boeing 767 for the price of 188 million USD each and have in our fleet 150 of such.

10. Not too many people know that Nigeria does not only assemble cars, but now manufactures own cars from scratch. These Nigerian manufactured vehicles are as good as Nissan's, Opel, or any foreign made cars. Innoson IVM pickup trucks is what our Nigerian Police uses today. At $20, 000 USD per truck, we could buy 1 million brand new trucks for the Nigerian police for the next 10 years. In such a case, crime will have no place in Nigeria.

11. With $200 billion USD we could pay the salary of our Youth Corps for the next 1,500 years, if each of them receives 20,000 Naira monthly.

12. $200 billion USD would provide 2 laptops for every Nigerian alive (170 million Nigerians). If the price of a laptop is 100 thousand naira.

13. When the tragedy of 9/11, 2001 happened in America, the whole world stood still because of its magnitude. But with $200 billion USD we can build 50 world trade centers. Because each one of the newly built ones cost 4 billion USD. That is to say we can have a world trade center in every state capital in Nigeria.

14. The most expensive car in the world cost 4 million USD, it is called Lamborghini Veneno.

With $200 billion USD you can buy 50,000 of such cars.

15. If the Nigerian president earns 12 million Naira monthly, with $200 billion USD we could pay him for over 2000 years.

16. With $200 billion USD, Nigeria could be having 10 Dangote companies if we assume he is worth $20 billion USD.

17. If a national stadium costs $50 million dollars to build, with $200 billion USD we could build a national stadium in every state and still have left overs.

18. With $200 billion USD, Nigeria could have 1000 F-35C lightning II fighter jets in their Air force. Each of the jets cost $200 million each.

19. With $200 billion USD Nigeria could own her own continent or Islands. The world's most expensive Island Lanai Island in Hawaii cost only $500 million dollars. We could purchase 400 of those islands and have 400 little countries under Nigeria.

20. If you were given $200 billion USD and you spent 1 million Naira an hour it would take you over 6 thousand years to spend it all.

What could these wasted funds have done, if well managed?

If Nigeria is losing about 400,000 barrels of oil per day to oil bunkering and spillage, what is the opportunity cost of that to the Nigerian economy?

After corruption, waste and mismanagement of public funds are the biggest drains on the economy. Even before the present economic downturn, reducing them had become imperative. Wastage is an important aspect of corruption we may be neglecting. Since no one claims responsibility for it, that is why few people hear of prosecutions. A clear case is the case of oil bunkering, spillage and gas flaring that has bedeviled the Nigerian economy.

Corruption appears to have taught us in Nigeria a strange lesson of how not to be honest, virtuous and law-abiding. It is fast looking like it does not pay to be honest and respect values. Through corrupt means, political office holders have acquired untold wealth within and without Nigeria and display such ostentatiously and the society celebrates them. Politicians also appear to have developed a business model of turning public office into investments.

Waste is the resultant effect of corruption. Corruption wastes skills; wastes time; wastes valuable resources and often compromise integrity. For instance, the International Monetary Fund (IMF) has withdrawn development aids from some countries on the basis of corruption. Like we said earlier, corruption is an enemy of development. In the next section we will be looking at the cost of waste especially in the oil industry where most of Nigeria's economic activities take place.

In a report by an international consulting firm, PwC, corruption in Nigeria could cost up to 37% of GDP by 2030 if it's not dealt with immediately. This cost is equated to around $1,000 per person in 2014 and nearly $2,000 per person by 2030. The boost in average income that was estimated, given the current per capita income, can significantly improve the lives of many in Nigeria.

OIL: THE WASTED MILLIONS

Those who have lived or worked with me know how much I hate wasting items. This, I think, is a habit we should teach our children. We must teach them not to waste food or things we buy for them. Once I quarreled with some of my family friends who came to stay with us one time over wasting food items. Some of the children grumbled, but the message was clear. There are children that do not have any to eat. As far as I am concerned, wasting items such as food does not mean you have abundance, it is also not a sign of how well you live but how unspiritual you are. God Himself does not like wastage. That was why after feeding the multitude with bread and fish, Jesus Christ instructed them to "gather the crumbs."

Staying with grandma while I was growing up, I discovered she almost never threw away anything. To her, nothing was a waste. She found use(s) for anything and everything. She was born and raised in the remotest and some of the poorest rural areas in the old Western Region in Nigeria. Her background of being raised in an environment of poverty shaped her ways of life that seems not to change.

Mama will keep all clothing items her children bought for her and keep the tags on the clothes. She will, after opening her birthday cake, keep the box and wrapping papers which meant much to her as the gift itself.

She will then dance around the gift item after keeping those things other people might have considered wastes. Grandma has a pile of new clothes her children bought for her, but she almost never wore them. Her kitchen utensil like knives reveals they need "retirement from active service." Many of them have worn thin obviously from years of excessive sharpening. The leftover food must be collected since her chickens will appreciate them. If a pair of shoes wore thin, she mended them. If they went beyond repair, she reserved them to be used as part of fuel for cooking in the next family party. For her, everything has a value, if not in one way, then in another.

Growing up, I found grandma's behavior so strange. But I learnt these lessons from her. The critical lesson is not to live a life of waste. As far as grandma was concerned, having more than enough does not mean one must waste things of value. Unfortunately, we are wasting a lot of resources today in Nigeria, yet we complain of not having enough!

There is never anything good about wasting your resources. Let us admit that mama is old school and therefore, maybe due to her rural upbringing, she had to "manage" all she had. Wastage is not even spiritual. Jesus Christ, after feeding the multitude with bread and fish issued the command to His disciples:

GATHER UP THE FRAGMENTS THAT REMAIN, SO THAT NOTHING IS LOST.

JOHN 6:12.

If Jesus Christ, with all the abundance of grace at his disposal, can frown against waste, then why should we not take His instructions to *"Gather up the fragments..."* of our resources so that *"nothing is lost."*?

One of the greatest news that has been heard on the African continent in the last decade, is the news of Ghana joining the league of oil producing nations. That singular discovery added so much to the Ghanaian economy that it catapulted Ghana's economy into one of the fastest growing in the world. It is believed that Ghana currently produces about 400,000 barrels of oil per day, which is equal to 40 million USD per day, based on the 2014 price of $100 per barrel.

Now, friends, this is where I want us to pay a very close attention. The same amount of money that has hugely enhanced the economy of Ghana, creating many opportunities and bringing joy to the lives and families of millions of Ghanaians, is the very same amount of crude oil value unaccounted for daily in Nigeria.

In the words of former Coordinating Minister of the Economy and the Minister of Finance Dr. (Mrs.)Ngozi Okonjo-Iweala while addressing the House of Representatives Joint Committee on Appropriation/Finance in Abuja in 2013 said, *"We are losing revenue; 400,000 barrels of crude oil are lost on a daily basis due to illegal bunkering, vandalism and production shut-in."*

That is the government official's way of saying that 400,000 barrels of oil is stolen daily in Nigeria. As of the year 2003 when oil was selling for way above $100, that could be anything between 40-50 million USD per day. Furthermore, if we count 5 working days, it makes 295 working days a year, which equals to 118 million barrels per year, which means $11.8 billion USD a year. This is only for the year 2013.

Before we go ahead, let us come out clear on a funda-mental point. I do not want anyone to think Pastor Sunday hates former President Jonathan or his admin-istration to the point of writing a whole book to attack him. Whenever I mention any name in this book, it is for clarification not condemnation. The election has come and gone. Let bygones be bygones. I am simply referring to his government as a matter of fact or reference not for accusation. My appeal to Nigerians is, let us move on.

If we are going to count how much was lost, only during the government of President Jonathan, then it becomes easy to believe the calculations done by the former Governor of the Central Bank of Nigeria (CBN) Prof. Chukwuma Soludo. He alleged that 30 trillion Naira (the equivalent of 200 billion USD in 2013) was lost to corruption in Nigeria. This is only in 6 years of President Jonathan's government, from the year 2009 – 2015.

To put that in perspective, the amount of money Nigeria lost in 6 years is bigger than the whole economy of the Ukraine $177 billion, Kuwait $175 billion, Libya $74 billion, Hungary $133 billion, Morocco $114 billion, Romania $189 billion, Belarus $71 billion, Syria $71 billion, Angola $124 billion and Vietnam $171 billion etc. according to the 2013 World Bank statistics for nominal GDP of countries.

Remember we are only talking about the amount Nigeria lost in the oil sector. Let me even make it clearer. According to the 2013 World Bank reports, that amount of $200 billion we lost in 6 years is 4 times the whole economy of Ghana $48 billion, 4 times that of Ethiopia

$47 billion, 4 times that of Tunisia $46 billion and Kenya $55 billion.

It gets more interesting, let me bring it closer to home and compare this amount to the GDP of some countries where Nigerians now run to as economic refugees. The lost $200 billion USD equivalent as at 2013 we are talking about is 6 times the budget of Cameroon $30 billion, 10 times the size of the economy of Zambia $20 billion, 10 times the economy of Uganda $19 billion, 10 times the economy of Gabon $19 billion, 14 times the economy of Senegal $14 billion, Botswana $14 billion, Jamaica $14 billion, republic of Congo $13 billion, equatorial Guinean $14 billion and Mozambique $14 billion according to World Bank GDP report of countries by 2013.

The amount we lost in 6 years is half of the whole economy (GDP) of South Africa, Denmark, Venezuela, Colombia, Thailand, Austria, Iran, United Arab Emirates, and Malaysia. Oh my God!!! What a country we would have built if not for the monster of corruption!

THE MISSING MILLIONS

It becomes more interesting when we do a thorough analysis of these missing millions. These figures are scary. Let us look at some even more daunting statistics of how corruption has eaten into the fabric of the Nigerian economy.

According to Mr. Obinna Akukwe a University of Nigeria, Nsukka (UNN) trained Financial, IT and Project Management Consultant and Adams Oshiomhole (a former Labor Leader for close to a decade) and Governor of Edo state, $27 billion that should be in excess crude account has been stolen. Oshiomhole once said that *"Nigeria's budgets for three years (2012 -2015) have been based on the average of $77 and $79, while the average price of the country's crude has been $108 per barrel, which gives an average surplus of $30 per barrel."* He said.

The governor continued, "Ideally, we ought to be saving $36 per barrel on the 2.3 million barrel a day over the past three years and if you look at these numbers you will find that what we have in our excess crude oil account should be over $30 billion but as we speak, we have barely $3 billion in our excess crude account."

Though the NNPC had agreed that under their watch, $11 billion was stolen or missing in 2013 alone, we shall still use the conservative figure of $5 billion annually to calculate the oil theft. The use of least average in cost computations is applied. The use of 60 months below is the amount of months President Jonathan's government was in charge of the purse of the Federal Republic of Nigeria.

1. Let us take the $20 billion missing or unaccounted for under the NNPC coffers since 2012. If we make these calculations for 18 months, we have a staggering $1.1 billion monthly (stolen or missing). If we take this for five years (or 60 months) we have the sum of $66 billion.

   What this means in simple English is that $66 billion added no value to the national GDP in the years under review. The money is either in private accounts in foreign banks or buried in inconspicuous buildings to prevent being detected by the authorities.

2. Taking the former Edo state Governor's claim that $30 per barrel above budget benchmark of $79 not accounted for, this means that for excess crude account we have a total sum of $27 billion in the period under review. I will save the effect of this for a later discussion in this book.

3. The Subsidy Probes in the House of Representatives have revealed that $5 billion is lost annually to oil thieves. This simply means $0.41 billion monthly. If we take this average for a period of five years (or 60 months) we should have $25 billion.

4. The Subsidy Probes have also revealed that wanton $1.5 billion were lost to suspicious waiver on petroleum products in 9 months. When this is calculated over the period of five years at $0.16 billion monthly we have $9.6 billion.

5. The 2011 Subsidy Scam reveals $6.8 billion was lost in revenue to unscrupulous and phony marketers and corrupt government officials and their cronies during the period.

6. In 2013, an audit on the NNPC account was carried out and discovered that monumental fraud took place. The Swiss-NNPC Oil Scam at the period shows a revenue loss of $6.8 billion.

7. Lastly, we must not forget the Malabu Oil Scam of 2011. This cost the nation the sum of $1 billion.

These figures, calculated at their minimum possible values shows us that a total probable missing/stolen or un-remitted oil funds in 60 months (our period under review) was $142.2 billion, in the most conservative estimation.

Let us not forget that this is the amount that could be logically traced according to the people mentioned above. In all, the total still comes to an average of $200 billion according to Prof. Soludo's account for the 6 years of President Jonathan's administration.

Throughout this book I will be using the amount of $200 billion that was lost between 2009 and 2015. This is because they are the biggest loses we recently suffered and was widely reported. Without talking about $20 trillion, $200 billion could have been used to bring about enormous development in Nigeria and you will see how as we go along.

Many of our lay readers may not understand these figures and what they mean in real terms. Let me put them in plain language for them to understand. I will try to paint a vivid picture of what $200 billion USD would mean so that it can be better appreciated.

1. If you were to put $200 billion one dollar bills end to end, you could make 20 round trips to the moon. You heard me right. You may have to read that again!

2. $200 billion could have translated into millions of vaccinations for children, which could have saved the lives of so many kids. There are too many children roaming the streets that need vaccinations and good health care and have been denied that.

A lot of children die daily from common diseases like malaria, cholera, and dysentery. Many are poorly fed. With $200 billion, we can turn things around for the future generation.

3. $200 billion could have become thousands of kilometers of roads constructed. Many of our roads in Nigeria are nothing but death traps. It is fast appearing that the safest mode of transportation in the country now is trekking. The air transport system is not so safe thanks to monumental corruption in the regulatory agencies. The rail system has been largely abandoned and it is at best, old fashioned. The roads are not fit for modern-day transport systems. We could have turned this around, if huge amounts of funds have not been stolen from our coffers!

4. $200 billion could have become thousands of schools built. There are too many children roaming the streets that need to go to school and get good education but have been denied it. With $200 billion, we could turn things around for the future generation.

5. $200 billion could have become thousands of hospitals in every town in Nigeria. In a country where the poor lack the resources to access modern health care facilities, building a well-furnished primary health care facility in every local government and town is not too much to ask for if $200 billion can be invested in it!

6. $200 billion could have become 100% water supply in all towns and villages of Nigeria. With many dying of water-borne diseases like typhoid, cholera and others, access to clean water in Nigeria can be a possibility if we invest $200 billion in it.

7. $200 billion could have resolved our electricity problem, giving us 100% supply to every home. It has been said that if we can fix the power sector in the country, about half of our problems have been solved: employment will be generated; more businesses will spring up; support services for businesses will be created and the GDP will be on the rise. Injecting the additional sum of $200 billion will make this happen.

8. As we speak, more than 20 of Nigeria's 36 states are presently struggling to pay salaries of workers. In fact, as I write (March, 2017), some have not paid their workers this year. The sum of $200 billion will pay the combined workers of Kwara, Ekiti and Enugu for a continuous period of over 60 years, if the minimum wage is N18,500 per worker and the number of workers are 1 million!

Need I say more?

Let me however remind you that we are only talking here of the money that is lost only in the oil sector of Nigeria.

Let's paint another picture. Dubai has become one of the wonders of the 21st century and the wonder of Dubai itself is called the Burj Khalifa building. It is the tallest building in the world measuring 2,723 ft. For comparison's sake, it was built for 1.5 billion USD, which is "chicken change" to our politicians in Nigeria.

If we are now saying, that in 6 years we lost 200 billion USD, with that amount of money judiciously used, every state capital in Nigeria will have its own Burj Khalifa building. That on its own would make Nigeria a tourist attraction, more than Dubai and maybe more than the United States of America. Nigeria only has 36 states. After constructing this massive structure in every state, we will still have enough money to build over 70 more of such structures.

What I am trying to say is that the harm corruption is doing to our country is so bad that I advocate for every Nigerian, at home and abroad, to join the crusade against this deadly practice in our nation. We have to fight it with everything we have. The magnitude of wastages of this nature is one major inhibition to Nigeria's economic growth.

CHAPTER FOUR

The Impacts of Corruption

CORRUPTION IS THE ENEMY OF DEVELOP-
MENT, AND OF GOOD GOVERNANCE. IT
MUST BE GOT RID OF. BOTH THE GOVERN-
MENT AND THE PEOPLE AT LARGE MUST
COME TOGETHER TO ACHIEVE THIS
NATIONAL OBJECTIVE.

PRATIBHA PATIL

In this chapter, we shall be looking at the devastating
effects of corruption. The multiple developmental problems confronting Nigeria today, is arguably the symptoms of bad governance characterized by institutionalized corruption. In his inaugural Presidential Address
on May 29, 1999, Chief Olusegun Obasanjo said: *"no
society can achieve anything near its full potentials if it
allows corruption to become the full-blown cancer that it
has become in Nigeria."* Also, one of the key campaign
promises and high points of the Buhari administration
is the spirited fight against corruption.

Many scholars seem to agree that corruption has
mainly destructive effects. Many studies have also been

conducted and found out that this destroys the economic life of the people; makes economic planning difficult; creates room for political and social instability; concentrates wealth in the hands of the few; promotes mediocrity, nepotism and inefficiency; stunts economic growth of the nation; promotes poverty and unemployment; compromises the electoral and other political processes; destroys democratic values; reduces regulations standards in public goods; pose threats to national integration and the likes.

In his wonderful book, Controlling Corruption, Robert Klitgaard writes: *"Systematic corruption distorts incentive, undermines institutions and redistributes wealth and power to the undeserving. Those who pay and receive bribes are expropriating a nation's wealth, leaving little for its poor citizens. When corruption undermines... economic and political developments are crippled."*

It is clear that corruption engenders the enthronement of bad and corrupt leadership, poor governance and ineffective administration. It diverts scarce resources into private accounts and thereby posing a threat to political stability. From what we can see, widespread corruption in governance makes it impossible for a leader to enlist support for development programs or to ask for sacrifices from his people for long term development. The people may simply hold the leader in contempt. The formidable opposition in some quarters especially from some civil society organizations and religious groups attests to this point.

The strangle-hold of corruption on a nation debases public morality and values. It engenders distrust towards public institutions. It distorts competition, thereby creating artificial monopolies. This can lead to over invoicing, wrong siting of public projects, lower standards in distribution of public goods and reduced public revenue generation.

CORRUPTION AND UNDERDEVELOPMENT

Empirical research carried out by two economists from the International Monetary Fund (IMF) Paolo Mauro[1] and Vivo Tanzi[2] suggests a strong connection between corruption and economic underdevelopment. These researchers who studied several countries as case studies to demonstrate that corruption especially are negatively correlated with economic growth. They concluded that a nation with so much potential in terms of economic resources tend to have stunted growth because of corruption. Paolo Mauro, for instance, found out that in corrupt societies, government functionaries tend to devote much of their time to competing for positions of economic power and in the pursuit of rents. This perennial rent-seeking activity not only erodes the capacity of public institutions to function properly, but greatly undermines economic development. The immediate impacts of corruption on development clearly manifest in a simple survey of the Niger Delta region of Nigeria, which accounts for the bulk of oil production in the country.

The Niger Delta region, the home of most of Nigeria's southern minority groups, harbors crude-oil reserves to, according to Sola Omotola[3], the tune of thirty-three billion barrels and natural-gas reserves of 160 trillion cubic feet. From oil alone, Nigeria generated roughly US$300 billion between 1970 and 2002, yet the Niger

Delta, where oil is extracted, remains underdeveloped and its inhabitants remain one of the poorest peoples of Nigeria. As a 2005 Amnesty International report confirms: *"In spite of windfall gains for the Nigerian government as global oil prices have more than doubled in the past two years, the inhabitants of the Niger Delta region remain among the most deprived oil communities in the world - 70 percent live on less than US$1 a day, the standard economic measure of absolute poverty".* Available figures, by the report of the Washington-based Environmental Change and Security Project[4] indicate that *"there is one doctor per 82,000 people, rising to one doctor per 132,000 people in some areas,"* especially the rural areas - which is more than three times the national average of 40,000 people per doctor. To make matters worse, only 27 percent of people in the region have access to safe drinking water, and only 30 percent of households have access to electricity - both of which proportions are below the national averages of 31.7 percent and 33.6 percent, respectively. For many people in the delta region, progress and hope, much less prosperity, remain out of reach.

The UNDP Niger Delta Human Development Report concludes that the Niger Delta region has *"an appalling human development situation summed up in social instability, poor local governance, neglect of infrastructure, lack of access to fundamental services, environmental degradation, and extreme economic deprivation".* This circumstance has resulted in a growing wave of mobilization and opposition by ethnic minority groups against their perceived marginalization, exploitation, and subjugation within the Nigerian federation: *"this ethnic minority ferment has engendered violent conflicts, involving thousands of fatalities,"* in the oil-producing parts of the region.

Crucially, there are three contending stakeholders in the Nigerian oil sector: the oil-bearing communities, the oil companies, and the political leadership at the Federal level. But there is a sense in which these stakeholders can be reduced to two. Indeed, what the region has experienced so far is the collusion of two players - the oil companies and the political leadership - against the oil-bearing communities. Increasingly, the line of demarcation between the oil multinationals and the political leadership has become blurred. This is because they seem united by a common purpose: to loot the resources dry. The net effect is that corruption has reduced according to two Nigerian scholars[5] *"the legitimacy of the leadership, eroded the credibility of political leaders, replaced merit and hard work with strong and complex patron-client relations, accentuated inefficiency, ineffectiveness, and general disorder in the bureaucratic apparatuses, and led to mismanagement, waste, and, ultimately, economic crisis."*

Many scholars have noted that all forms of corruption are deceits, lies that sacrifice the common good or the public interest for something much less. It deviates from the search for the Good Society and, instead, emboldens social pathologies. Not only does it point society to the wrong path, but it exhausts and erodes governmental legitimacy, supports the wrong kind of public leadership, and sets the wrong kind of footprints for present and future generations. It prevents the public realm from pursuing the general welfare. The adverse effects of corruption in any corruption-plagued society, like Nigeria, are well documented:

1. Corruption undermines political decisions, leads to inefficient use of resources, and benefits the unscrupulous at the cost of the law abiding.

2. Corruption involves the loss of moral authority, weakens the efficiency of government operations, increases opportunities for organized crime, encourages police brutality, adds to taxpayers' burdens, and affects the poor directly.

3. Corruption is something everybody pays for at a huge cost, direct and indirect. It is public-works development that people do not want. It is shoddy construction which becomes rapidly obsolete and therefore needs to be redone. It is public money used to fund inflated contracts or to replace skimmed revenues. It is buildings which threaten public health and safety.

4. Corruption allows immunity for criminal acts so that the law is for sale to the highest bidder. If left unchecked, corruption will eventually result in a "softness of state," comprising all manner of social indiscipline that prevents effective government and impedes national development. Nigeria is an unenviable testimony.

5. It reduces the chances of the nation getting foreign investments. Foreign direct investment (FDI) is discouraged by high corruption levels. Corruption acts like a tax on FDI. Studies[6] have

shown that corruption discourages investments. Though some may argue that China, Brazil, Thailand and Mexico attract large flows of FDI despite their perceived high corruption, high corruption levels would have attracted more FDI if corruption had been lower.

How Corruption Kills Nigeria

Having looked at the relationship between corruption and underdevelopment, we can see that the case of Nigeria shows that the country has refused to develop simply because of corruption. It is because of corruption:

1. We don't have enough universities to admit our teeming young population into different courses of study. As a result, our young men and women (teenagers especially) are scattered all over the world looking for admissions and spending billions of parental hard earned money in the process. The multiplier effect of this is brain drain and lack of patriotism among our youths.

2. The fact that we have few universities itself is bad enough. That we do not have quality and up-to-date equipment for our teachers in the universities is equally frustrating. Because of corruption, our teachers and professors cannot be properly paid. The numerous strikes by the Academic Staff Union of Universities (ASUU) and other unions over their remunerations and emoluments are some of the direct effects of bureaucratic corruption. Many of our students

are made to spend longer years on campuses due to frequent closures and strikes by the university teachers. Some of these young ones, have resorted to drugs, prostitution, and other vices as a result of prolonged closures of the campuses. Poor payment of teachers; several industrial crisis in the University system on issues bothering on delays or non-payment of salaries; poor research outputs; low motivation to work on the part of teachers; cultism and drug abuse in institutions of higher learning and the likes are the remote and immediate causes of corruption in the educational sector.

3. A drive around several parts of the country will reveal several "uncompleted" government projects like abandoned roads, buildings and other infrastructure. One will see that both large and middle scale projects are left uncompleted; buildings, airports, highways, hospitals, stadiums etc. litter the whole country. The multi-billion naira Ajaokuta Steel in Kogi state built with the support from Russian government have been largely abandoned. This is a project that, if completed, Nigeria should have no business with oil anymore. But who will tell them?

4. In Nigeria today, millions of children are dying of malnutrition and lack of food. I watched the pathetic state of living in the Internally Displaced Persons (IDPs) camps across the nation on television the other day and I felt like shedding tears. Even for other people's misfortune, some people

have become billionaires. There have been reports of shady deals by some Non-Governmental Organizations (NGOs) and individuals feeding fat on the misfortunes of the IDPs. Food items donated by donor agencies have been reported syphoned or diverted into private pockets. All these because of limited economic gains!

5. So many families go to bed on empty stomachs. In Nigeria today, hunger keeps a lot of families as companions. In fact, they have hunger as a constant companion. Some families cannot have 3 square meals in a day. In a country where most people live on less than one dollar a day, two square meals must be considered a luxury. All these have their roots in corruption and misman-agement of state resources.

6. Our maternal and child-mortality rate is one of the highest in the world because of our substan-dard medical services. In Nigeria today, it will surprise anyone who left the country over 30 years ago who came back visiting that there are still overcrowded hospitals; poor medical atten-tion; overworked medical personnel; unavail-ability of drugs and up-to-date equipment; and the likes are some of the symptoms of corruption in the health sector.

7. Our roads claim thousands of lives each year because of their deplorable state. As a result of poor regulations and reduction in standards, road contractors do shabby jobs and pass as

"completed projects" simply because there are poor inspections, regulation enforcement and lack of due processes. Social amenities and infrastructure: lack of facilities for sporting events; abandoned projects; deplorable roads and networks and the likes are the effects of corruption on social services.

8. As strange as it looks, corruption sends true investors away. Real investors want value for money not simply short cuts. It costs more to operate in a corrupt environment. If at every point, an investor will have to "settle" someone or some people for them to do their jobs, the chances are that they either stay back to do substandard jobs to cover their cost of capitals or simply look for some other saner environments were business can be done in a friendly manner. These are ways investors are kept out of our economy. The likes of Dunlop, Mouka Foam, and many others left partly because of corruption. Poor investors' confidence: as a result of corruption, the propensity to invest in the economy will be low.

9. The actions of militant groups in the Niger delta and even such deadly organization as Boko Haram, Kidnappings, human trafficking and the likes are all fueled directly or indirectly by corruption. The renewed blowing up of pipelines in the Niger-Delta; poor police remunerations; rise in insurgent attacks; land crisis between herdsmen and farmers are fallouts of the effects of corruption.

As I go into talking about why I believe Nigeria's economy would eventually overtake America's economy, let me first of all give you a picture of what the stolen or "missing" USD $ 200 billion could have done positively to Nigerians.

1. It will cost us about $1 billion or less to generate 1000 Mega Watts (MW) of a gas power electricity plant. With $200 billion USD we could produce enough electricity to rival any developed country. For example South Africa produces just over 40,000 MW. The same is true of the United Kingdom (UK). We should be able to produce 4 times that amount, and with electricity, our development would be hugely accelerated. In fact, if that same amount of money is invested in our energy sector, Nigeria will achieve what I call "overnight economic development."

2. With $200 billion USD, we will provide safe and clean water to the entire world for 20 years. At an estimated population of 8 billion people and the cost of providing water for the world per year being USD $10 billion we can achieve this feat.

3. The sum of $200 billion USD can provide MMR vaccine for every child in the world, 20 times over. The nuisance of polio and other children diseases will be eradicated with that sum alone.

4. With $200 billion USD we can afford the payment for the registration of all aspiring Nigerian youths who want to register for the West African Examination Council (WAEC) and Unified Tertiary

Matriculation Examination (UTME) at the rate of 25, 000 Naira per student. At an estimated population of 70 million youths, it could pay for them for 20 years consecutively.

5. With $200 billion USD we can sponsor the whole United Nations relief operation for 15 years consecutively, bearing in mind that for the year 2014 the budget for relief operation was $13 billion USD.

6. With $200 billion USD we could feed the entire Nigeria population of 170 million people free for 10 months. The cases of malnutrition and associated diseases can be eradicated from our land with that sum.

7. The biggest banks in Nigeria, for example First Bank or Zenith Bank are priced at $20 billion dollars. We could have 10 more of those banks. These will create thousands of additional jobs for our teeming youths.

8. With $200 billion USD we could sponsor over 2000 Nigerians mission to Mars. If India spent 75 million USD on their mission to Mars, imagine what $200 billion USD will do?

9. With $200 billion USD we could rebuild Nigerian Airways and equip it with the latest Boeing 767 for the price of $188 million USD each and have in our fleet 150 of such.

10. Not too many people know that Nigeria does not only assemble cars, but now manufactures own cars from scratch. These Nigerian manufactured vehicles are as good as Nissan's, Opel, or any foreign made cars. Innoson IVM pickup trucks is what our Nigerian Police uses today. At $20, 000 USD per truck, we could buy 1 million brand new trucks for the Nigerian police for the next 10 years. In such a case, crime will have no place in Nigeria.

11. With $200 billion USD we could pay the salary of our National Youth Service Corps (NYSC) members for the next 1,500 years, if each of them receives 20,000 Naira monthly.

12. Every Nigerian can be provided with at least a laptop with $200 billion USD at an estimated 170 million population if we take the price of a laptop to be N100, 000.

13. When the tragedy of September 11, 2001 happened in America, the whole world stood still because of its magnitude. But with $200 billion USD we can build 50 World Trade Centers. Each one of the newly built ones cost $4 billion USD. That is to say we can have a world trade center in every state capital in Nigeria had $200 billion USD been put to effective use.

14. The most expensive car in the world cost 4 million USD, it is called Lamborghini Veneno. With $200 billion USD you can buy 50,000 of such cars.

15. If the Nigerian president earns 12 million Naira monthly. With $200 billion USD we could pay him for over 2000 years.

16. With $200 billion USD, Nigeria could be having 10 Dangote companies if we assume he is worth $20 billion USD.

17. If it costs $50 million USD to build a national stadium, with $200 billion USD we could build a national stadium in every state and still have left overs.

18. With $200 billion USD, Nigeria could have 1000 F-35C lightning II fighter jets in their Air force. Each of the jets cost $200 million each.

19. With $200 billion USD Nigeria could own her own continent or Islands. The world's most expensive Island Lanai Island in Hawaii cost only $500 million dollars. We could purchase 400 of those islands and have 400 little countries under Nigeria.

20. If you were given $200 billion USD and you spent 1 million Naira an hour it would take you over 6 thousand years to spend it all.

THE CUMULATIVE IMPACT OF CORRUPTION IN NIGERIA

The fraudulent accumulation process has resulted, over time, in the progressive and phenomenal enrichment of Nigerian leaders (both civilian and military), the looting of the national treasury and the indebtedness of the country almost to the point of bankruptcy: hence the critical dearth of resources for investment on the social, economic and overall cultural development of the masses of our people. Nigeria is, therefore, in a paradoxical situation in which the scandalous, almost legendary, wealth of key ruling class members exists to mock the unspeakable mass poverty, misery and degradation of the Nigerian people. This has, in turn brought about a situation of potential and actual violent confrontation between the minority plutocrats and the majority paupers and destitute; within which context the current urban phenomenon of 'area boys' is just a minor manifestation. This situation is also highly productive, at the attitudinal level, of mass cynicism about, and distrust of the political elite, and constitutes a major factor in the persistence of inter- and intra-communal disunity, antipathy and strife, as well as the progressively worsening problem of political and social instability since independence. Since the public treasury has been the primary and ultimate source of rapid and sensational private accumulation by the Nigerian political elite, the struggle to capture state power (and, therefore, the national treasury) among factions of the ruling class has become progressively acrimonious and bitter. This is because in this kind of struggle which ends in a winner-take-all resolution, the losing factions tend to be rigorously excluded from sharing in the loot. Hence, the invariable tendency among elite factions to use the poor masses from their areas of origin (village, town, local government, state or ethnic group) as cannon fodder and battering rams against their rivals and competitors from other areas, thus further dividing the people and undermining the stability in Nigerian that is already profoundly unstable.

Rampant corruption among the ruling class has, over time, taught a dangerously disruptive lesson to the generality of the people: being honest and law-abiding does not pay. Consequently some of the ordinary people who have learnt this lesson from the top then try to replicate the corrupt practices of their leaders at their own lowly levels in the form of petty acts of bribery, peculation and embezzlement of public funds. It is in this way that corruption as a way of life has become pervasive and popularized in the Nigerian society where the working people's real incomes have become so devalued that it is impossible for most salary and wage earners and those on marginal and inelastic incomes to survive on their legitimate earnings.

The obsession of many of our political leaders with primitive private accumulation at the expense of the public means that they tend to divert resources earmarked for running and maintaining public institutions in their charge (institutions like hospitals, schools, universities, public utilities, the judiciary, the police and even the armed forces) to corrupt private purposes. By so doing, they subvert these institutions and their capacity to perform their assigned tasks efficiently, thereby damaging the substantive interests and endangering the lives of citizens whom these public institutions are meant to serve. Through the systematic pillage of the nation's wealth by its supposed custodians over several decades, many young Nigerians of lowly origins, after successfully passing out of schools, universities and other institutions of learning, cannot find gainful employment. This is because resources, which could have been used for job creation, have been looted by the leaders. As a consequence many of these educated young people are either 'brain drained' to other lands in search of greener pastures, or get diverted into various criminal ways of making a livelihood like armed robbery, prostitution, drug peddling and trafficking and all manner of racketeering. In this and other ways, greedy Nigerian leaders have squandered the future of their country and its children, and reduced Nigeria to its present status of a pariah in the comity of nations.

I hope everyone reading this would now understand the reason for my tenacious and relentless campaign for us to have a new government in Nigeria. I hope you can now understand why religious arguments and sentiments did not derail me from seeing a worthy government take over our nation's leadership. My firm position is dictated by what I know. That is why I will not allow less informed minds to sway my informed position.

I hope those well-wishers and friends that were telling me not to abandon my calling would now realize the reasons for my passion. I hope those who were lecturing me not to leave the pulpit now know better. I hope those who in good faith were encouraging me to simply devote myself to only preaching the gospel could now realize what a waste it could have been if I had been locked up in the pulpit. What could have become of me, my ministry and legacy, if I had not developed my capacity out of the box the way I have done over the past 30 years.

What I am doing now with Nigeria, I have done for countries all over the world. It is only now that I have decided to bring my wealth of experience to help my country Nigeria. I hope my people will listen to this cry from the wilderness afar off.

In the next chapter, we will be discussing the importance of curbing corruption and what it portends for our economy.

CHAPTER FIVE

Curbing Corruption

I am aware some people, even having read this book to this point still are not so convinced we can actually overtake the American economy. We must admit it is a herculean task. But here comes the key - READ ON!

If there is a short cut on how the Nigerian economy can overtake the American economy, it has to be in our deliberate resolve to curb corruption. This is the master key and the central thesis of this book.

Corruption, like we have established in previous chapters, is like cancer to the human body. We noted that it kills, it deforms, it disfigures, and it inhibits growth. This explains why when tumor is discovered, a good medical practitioner does everything it can to prevent its malignant growth. If not, it spreads to essential parts of the body and becomes too difficult to control.

Since cancer is not known to have a medical cure, the best a medical practitioner can do is to curb it for the organism to be able to live life to the fullest.

In this chapter, we shall be taking a good look at what we will be gaining by effectively curbing corruption.

FROM MISSING MILLIONS TO TRILLIONS

When something is not curbed, there are bigger chances it will do bigger damages. Previously, we were dealing with "missing millions and billions" now we have to cope with the reality of our missing trillions!

I want to take you back to the very same point I made in the beginning of this book to prove the fact that Nigeria actually went from stealing millions into trillions of US dollars. However as horrible as this looks, it is this very fact that provides us with the proofs that Nigeria has the potential to rival any country in the world. Please take your time to look at the figures below again.

The question had always been whether Nigeria can ever come to the same level with the United States of America (USA), which is the strongest economy in the world. There have been articles, books and in some cases conferences organized for this express purpose.

About $20-trillion had been stolen from Nigeria's coffers by leaders who had access to the nation's money between 1960 and 2005. This was disclosed by Dapo Olorunyomi, chief of staff to the chairman of the Economic and Financial Crimes Commission (EFCC) at a function in Lagos. Olorunyomi, who was speaking at the yearly Dinner/Re-union of the Lagos State chapter of the University of Ilorin Alumni Association, said the figure was sourced from the records of the United Nations Development Program (UNDP). (Reference: http://nigeriavillagesquare.com/forum/threads/efcc-says-nigerian-leaders-stole-20-trillion-in-45-years.5322/.)

This report was confirmed by a leading Nigerian newspaper The Vanguard from their publication on

March 25th 20015. (Reference: http://www.vanguardngr.
com/2015/03/20trn-stolen-from-from-nigerias-trea-
sury-by-leaders-efcc/)

Please pay attention to the above statement once again
and I will like you to read it over and over again. Because
of how incredible this might sound, I have endeavored
to provide the link and to confirm the sources of the
information. Please note that the Nigerian Economic
and Financial Crimes Commission is probably the
most reputed and most credible institution in Nigeria.
But besides that they don't want us to just believe their
report, even they are referring us to a more reputable
international organization in the United Nations Development Program (UNDP). The reason this is important
is because our international readers might find it difficult
to believe that such an amount as much as $20 trillion
dollars could even be generated in Nigeria to start with,
talk less of so much being stolen. To an average Nigerian
however, this is not news. They won't find it outrageous
to believe that Nigeria is that rich. In fact most Nigerians
know that their leaders have stolen more than $20 tril-
lion from the country's coffers.

Oxfam an international confederation of 20 NGOs
working with partners in over 90 countries to end the
injustices that cause poverty is another source that has
confirmed the report from the Economic and Financial
Crimes Commission (EFCC) and the United Nations
Development Programme (UNDP). In the words of their
representative, Mr Celestine Odo, of Good Governance
Program Coordinator for Oxfam, said that according to
the report, public office holders stole an estimated $20
trillion from the treasury between 1960 and 2005, while

multinational companies receive tax incentives esti-mated at $2.9bn a year.

Now what is $20 trillion USD? I have decided to illus-trate it to you below so that it can be easily fathomed and believed.

Talking about $20 trillion USD, remember that the Nigerian economy is presently worth only $510 billion USD. For your information the whole European Union is worth only between 17- 20 trillion USD. That is talking about all the 28 countries that are part of the European Union. America which is the single richest country in the world is worth 16-17 trillion USD by GDP as of 2013. At the same time China's GDP was worth 10 trillion USD and Japan 4-5 trillion USD.

Now my friends, I'm sure you can see where I deduced my argument from, that Nigeria's economy can still outgrow America's economy. If the total worth of the American economy today is 16-17 trillion USD by the GDP 2013 and the amount of money stolen from Nigeria in the past 50 years is $20 trillion USD. It means that Nigeria and Africa in general is indeed a wealthy conti-nent that could become the future economic giant of the world, if we could only get it right. The first thing we must get right is declaring war against corruption. From there, we can begin to put our resources into building a modern and civilized nation and continent. Note that the $20 trillion USD that has been stolen is talking about all the money stolen from all other economic sectors not just oil (including agriculture, finance, natural resources etc.). It is also important to note that this is within the first 45 years of Nigeria's independence. Nigeria is indeed a blessed nation. We are potentially wealthy in all aspects of life. But to preserve and actualize this wealth we all must join the anti-corruption brigade. More so, we all must hate corruption with a passion. We should all support the new government anyway possible to make sure that their campaign promises to fight corruption is fulfilled.

FIGHTING CORRUPTION IS NOT JUST GOOD GOVERNANCE. IT'S SELF-DEFENSE. IT'S PATRIOTISM.

JOE BIDEN

If Nigeria would successfully annihilate corruption in our society, we have enough resources, zeal, passion, and enthusiasm to take Nigeria to a new level of economic development. Our greatest resource is our people. Again allow me to say that from all my years of experience and traveling all over the world, I have become convinced that there is no group of people like Nigerians.

The zeal and enthusiasm of Nigerians is without comparison. Hardly can you find a people with such amount of zest, fervency, gusto, spirit and commitment as Nigerians.

Indeed this is NIGERIA - GOOD PEOPLE, GREAT NATION, in the words of the late Prof. Dora Akunyili.

The Economic and Financial Crimes Commission (EFCC) was set up by the Obasanjo administration to study, research, investigate and prosecute all forms of corruption related activities and financial crimes. It is one of the most feared and reputed institutions in the Nigerian society today. This is especially true under the leadership of its first chairman, the very young and zealous, Mallam Nuhu Ribadu.

I am going to base my argument in this section on figures of corruption in the Nigerian economy, provided by the EFCC under the leadership of Mallam Nuhu Ribadu. This research has proven why I believe Nigeria's economy will outperform America's economy, in the case that we put our acts together in fighting corruption.

According to the EFCC about $20 trillion USD has been stolen from the treasury by leaders who had access to the nation's money between 1960 - 2005. Please note that this does not include the 6 years under the leadership of President Jonathan, which has been much of our focus in this book.

Now what is $20 trillion USD? I would not even take my time or your time to begin to explain to you what this translates to in economic terms. I decided to illustrate for you above only what you could easily fathom and believe. Hence my focus was on the $200 billion USD that we lost in the past few years.

Talking about $20 trillion USD however, remember that the Nigerian economy is presently worth only $510 billion USD. For your information the whole European Union (EU) is worth only between 17 - 20 trillion USD. That is talking about all the 28 countries that are part of the European Union. America which is the single richest country in the world is worth 16 -17 trillion USD by GDP as of 2013. At the same time China's GDP was worth 10 trillion USD and Japan 4-5 trillion USD.

Now my friends, I'm sure you can see where I deduced my argument from, that Nigeria's economy can still outgrow America's economy. If the total worth of the American economy today is 16-17 trillion USD by the GDP 2013 and the amount of money stolen from Nigeria in the past 50 years is $20 trillion USD. It means that Nigeria and Africa in general is indeed a wealthy continent that could become the future economic giant of the world, if we could only get it right. The first thing we must get right is declaring war against corruption. From there, we can begin to put our resources into building a modern and civilized nation and continent.

Note that the $20 trillion USD that has been stolen is talking about all the money stolen from all other economic sectors not just oil (including agriculture, finance, natural resources etc.). It is also important to note that this is within the first 45 years of Nigeria's independence.

PREVIOUS ATTEMPTS AT CURBING CORRUPTION

While we have said over $20 trillion USD has either been stolen or missing from public coffers in Nigeria in the last fifty or more years, it will be totally untrue to say that there have been no attempts at curbing corruption.

With the open looting of the country's resources by politicians in the First Republic, not many were surprised that the first Military coup, in 1966, became the main check to the cankerworm of corruption at the time. Unfortunately, the military that was supposed to serve as a healer to the disease of corruption too became engulfed in corruption. We can classify these as extra-constitutional measures!

Aside extra-constitutional measures, there are other measures that have been adopted by various political regimes to fight corruption. We have had legal measures too. There have been several edicts, Acts of Parliaments and Decrees in Nigerian's law books designed specifically to curb corruption. We have had legislations and enactments like the Code of Conduct Bureau introduced under the 1979 Constitution, Advanced Free Fraud (also known as 419) Decree and the likes all to prevent graft. The Obansanjo administration promulgated the Anti-Corruption Act which established the Independent Corrupt Practices and Other related offences Commission (ICPC). The Failed Bank Decree alone has exposed massive cases of corruption in the private sector of the economy.

The second measures have been those dealing with creations of institutions dedicated to attitudinal changes. There have been massive educational and re-orientation programs on the destructive effects of corruption on the economy. We have had programs like "Ethical Revolution", Mass Mobilization for Social and Economic Reconstruction (MAMSER), the National Orientation Agency (NOA) under Babangida. The Buhari military administration established the War Against Indiscipline (WAI) to effect behavioral changes among Nigerians especially on corruption. Many who were alive in the 1980s, the fear of WAI Brigades located at public institutions and schools made everyone gear up.

The Murtala-Obasanjo regime made good their promise to hand over power to democratically-elected civilians in 1979. The circumstances and conditions under which the politicians of the Second Republic came to power on 1 October 1979 ensured that they would put corrupt enrichment at the very top of their political agenda. Among these circumstances and conditions was the peculiar constitutional order, mid-wived by the Constituents Assembly set up by the regime, and governing such aspects of political life as registration of national political parties and election to various offices at all levels of government. The constitutional provisions governing the formation and registration of political parties, and election to public offices on the platform of the registered parties were such that nobody could hope to be elected to any public office without a huge financial outlay, which was often several times larger than the total legitimate remuneration which a successful candidate could reasonably expect to earn in his or her four-year tenure in office. Since most members of the Nigerian political elite were not known to be motivated by anything but the crudest business considerations of how to maximize their profit from holding public offices, it became a matter of urgent necessity for them rapidly to recoup the capital outlay on their elections and show substantial profit on their investment. The strategy used by the politicians of the Second Republic to recoup their losses, while extending and consolidating their accumulative base, amounted to the refurbishing, combining and enlarging of all the known techniques of primitive accumulation previously practiced in Nigeria. These ranged from spurious and grossly inflated contracts and consultancies, import license racketeering, the presidential task force on rice importation, a multi-billion pound sterling commodity scam with the Johnson-Mathey Bank (JMB) of London, and the huge National Youth Service (NYSC) rip-off, to the unabashed looting by National and State Assemblymen in the form of grossly inflated salaries and allowances for maintaining non-existent aides and constituency offices, or irrelevant and irresponsible travelling expenses to exotic and far-flung parts of the globe.

A brand new addition to the politician's formidable arsenal for looting the resources of Nigeria was the pervasive practice whereby the executive arm of government at the state or federal level appointed liaison officers specifically to lobby members of the legislative arm, irrespective of party affiliation, to support legislative projects sponsored by the executive arm in the legislative assembly. Each legislative project was negotiated in turn between the executive's lobbyists and the legislators and the latter's consent for supporting the project was secured either with the payment of a substantial cash settlement to the legislator concerned or the award of a substantial government contract, including contracts to lift crude petroleum. As a consequence of this squander mania of epic proportions, which coincided with a sharp decline in Nigeria's oil revenue from 1981, the governments of the Second Republic found the somewhat reduced national income inadequate for their own private accumulative project. Consequently, they borrowed a leaf from their immediate predecessor, the Obasanjo government, and proceeded to boost the external debt stock of Nigeria from the 1979 level of $6.8 billion, according to the Central Bank of Nigeria, to about $15 billion when the military under Buhari/Idiagbon seized power again on December, 31st 1983.

This heavy borrowing on the Euro-dollar market facilitated the spending extravaganza for which the governments of the Second Republic became notorious. This in turn dramatically boosted the capacity of influential individual politicians to embark on corrupt, even

criminal enrichment. There was a rise of an unprecedented large number of emergency Nigerian millionaires
with their profusion of private jet planes, stately homes
at home, in Britain, other places in Europe and North
America, extremely expensive limousines and regular
lavish and bacchanalian parties. The essential corruption of Second Republic politicians could be gauged by
the fact that, while all this was going on, some of the
state governments claimed that they had no money to
pay salaries and wages to civil servants, teachers and
other public service workers for months on end.

In view of the foregoing, it was not surprising that
the government of the Second Republic rapidly lost
public credibility and support, or that the Nigerian
people received with relief, even joy, news of the Buhari/
Idiagbon coup that toppled the Second Republic on
December, 31st,1983.

The twenty-month Buhari/Idiagbon regime which
succeeded the Second Republic was distinguished by its
stern, even harsh response to the twin ills of corruption
and indiscipline among the public officers of the Second
Republic. Several top functionaries at Federal and State
levels were incarcerated for almost the whole tenure
of the regime without being charged or tried for any
offence, while some were tried secretly by special military tribunals and sentenced to long terms of imprisonment, including life, for crimes ranging from 'unlawful
enrichment' to 'contributing to the economic adversity
of the country'. Furthermore, the regime mounted a
public propaganda war against corruption and indiscipline (WAI) complete with a special paramilitary squad
for its execution known as the WAI brigade.

The regime raised the moral tone of the country because its anti-corruption campaign which coincided with the inner wishes of most Nigerians and also because the minority agents of corruption were intimidated into lying low by the regime's reputation for exacting harsh and exemplary penalties. By the end of its first year, however, the Buhari administration's anti-corruption campaign seemed to have run out of steam, partly because of the subversive activities of 'fifth columnists' within the regime being the leading 'fifth columnist'. For the twenty months of the regime's stay in power, and for his own subsequent eight years of unmitigated autocratic rule, Babangida never took a public stand against corruption. On the contrary, IBB's primary target of verbal and physical attack was what he identified early in 1984 as 'undue radicalism' or 'extremism'. But the main reason for the loss of steam of the Buhari regime's campaign against corruption and indiscipline was the regime's inability to deal effectively with the problem of economic and social decline inherited from the preceding regime. The regime also shot itself in the foot by trying to arrest the country's economic and social decline by doctrinaire and anti-people policies like massive retrenchment of workers in the public service, the introduction of many new taxes, levies and fees on citizens, drastic reduction in public expenditure, especially on social welfare and agricultural subsidies, and the widespread destruction of the means of livelihood of small privately employed persons like motor mechanics, food vendors and petty traders by pulling down their makeshift sheds, kiosks and bukas in the name of urban environmental sanitation.

Thirdly, there have been several probes and Inquiries in response to specific instances of corruption in Nigeria. We have had the African Continental Bank probe in 1957; the Coker Inquiry in 1962; Scania probe in 1969; Belgore cement probe in 1975; Civil Service purge in 1975; several NNPC probes since the 1980s and various military tribunals under the Buhari/Idiagbon regime in 1984.

Our immediate reaction to all these measures at curbing corruption is not that there has been lack of political will to fight corruption, but the general lack of interest from the Nigerian public.

At this juncture, I will like to point out a major mistake that the Nigerian public is making when it comes to corruption. We often leave the fight against corruption in the hands of the government it is high time he Nigerian population realizes and admits to the fact that it is only popular demand and national collective effort that can put an end to corruption. Every citizen of Nigeria needs to join the fight. The fight against corruption cannot be won by the government alone. It is a fight that must involve every conscientious Nigerian.

I will like to use this medium to appeal to every Nigerian to think of a way that he or she could contribute to the fight against corruption. Awareness is one of the major ways to stop the cancer of corruption. Every Nigerian should find the time and take the necessary efforts to spread the awareness of the dangers of corruption. It is my personal conviction that we need at least a million Nigerians actively campaigning against corruption on a daily basis before we can reduce the effect of corruption in our society.

I will especially like to challenge the young people to go ahead and spearhead this move. Let's go ahead and start hundreds and thousands of NGOs, pressure groups, civil societies. Until this becomes a mass movement. We will always lose the fight against corruption. This is one important lesson that must be drummed into the ears of every Nigerian. That if we are to become the country that we dream of having, it will take an effort to fight corruption from each and every one of us.

There is a seeming comfort with or lack of enthusiasm about the fight against corruption among Nigerians. The experience of Justice Kayode Esho's led National Committee on Corruption and Other Economic Crimes in the 1990s provides the key. In coming out with its report Prince Bola Ajibola, SAN, stated as follows:

"The response was not much. Only one of all the Chief Justices gave a reply to the appeal. Regrettably, there was response from only one of the [21] States' Attoneys-General. The Commissioner of Police of Ogun state sent a memorandum urging the pruning down of the various sections on corruption in our codes. Apart from this Command, no police Command nor the office of the Inspector General of Police responded to our call." (Report of the National Committee on Corruption and Other Economic Crimes, 1990: 3)

With responses like this, one can easily draw the following conclusions:

1. There is no corruption in the society or if there is, there is no need for a serious reaction to an anti-corruption call;

2. Corruption has become so ubiquitous that it is now a "normal" aspect of social life.

In our view, the second view seems to capture the reality of corruption in Nigeria today. This explains why we need the men and women to fix these institutions to fight corruption.

In fact, President Obama made the point clearly on his visit to Ghana in 2009 that Africa needs strong institutions and not men and women. If I am on the same page with these people, the word 'institution' is to be taken literarily as an organization that has a particular purpose. This may mean courts, parliaments, bureaucracies, political parties, electoral bodies, etc. If those are examples of institutions, then we have them in excess in Nigeria. To fight corruption alone, we have the Economic and Financial Crimes Commission (EFCC), the Independent Corrupt Practices and other related offences Commission (ICPC), the Code of Conduct Bureau, National Agency for Food, Drugs Administration and Control (NAFDAC), State Security Service (SSS), the Police, etc. Have the existence of these bodies reduced corruption in Nigeria?

It is on that note that I found another meaning of the word in Oxford Dictionary as: a person who is well known because s/he has been on a job for a long time. In the United States' Federal Reserve Board we can mention institutions like William M. Martin Jr., who served as chairman between 1951 and 1970 under five different administrations, both Democratic and Republican. Also we have Allan Greenspan, who was appointed chairman in 1987 and served four different Presidents, including

Bill Clinton, even though he himself was a Republican. These are institutions per excellence. And these we need.

When I hear people talk of 'institutions', they say it as though they will be manned by robots or X-Men. Judges can be bribed, influenced or intimidated; security agencies can be compromised; and other institutions can be deliberately underfunded (all these we recently witnessed in Nigeria). The reason for all these is that these institutions are manned by weak men. Weak men cannot rise above partisanship, tribalism, nepotism, ethnicity or religious bigotry.

Please, friends, do not get me wrong. Strong institutions are good, but without strong men, institutions will be weak!

THE WAY FORWARD ON CURBING CORRUPTION

It is my considered judgment that the primary reason why all attempts at curbing corruption in Nigeria have so far failed is that, while corruption has been deeply entrenched in the structures of the Nigerian state and society, all the advertised measures for combating it are conceived and operated at the level of form and symbolism. As long as the inequitable structures of a dependent neo-colonial state are allowed to reproduce in every generation a rampaging bourgeoisie of army officers, politicians, bureaucrats, businessmen, academics and touts whose raison d'etre is primitive accumulation and maximum consumption of imported luxuries, so long will all the formal institutions and measures for combating corruption (like judicial commissions of enquiry, Code of Conduct Bureau, Public Complaints

Commission, MAMSER, NOA, WAI fail to make any significant impact on the problem. This is because, by the structural logic of the monopoly of state power in Nigeria by the ruling class, all these institutions set up to deal with the problem of corruption are inevitably manned, controlled and operated by, and in the interest of, members of this ruling class who have a vested and entrenched interest in sustaining and even extending corrupt practices.

Consequently these putative warriors against corruption perform their task in such a way that they end up covering up rather than exposing corruption, thus helping to consolidate and perpetuate its hold on the society. One clever methodology for covering up the deeds of corrupt public officers probed by judicial commissions of enquiry was invented during the Obasanjo regime and developed to the status of an art during the Babangida regime. By this methodology the government appoints a supposedly high-powered judicial commission to investigate a notorious case of public corruption or misconduct and, after the commission has completed its work and submitted its report, the government either completely suppresses it, or in a few cases, merely publishes its own views on the report in form of a government 'white paper'. This so-called 'white paper' usually ignores all the serious and weighty findings and recommendations of the commission while highlighting only the trivial and innocuous ones which cannot in any way hurt government's cronies and agents who are the subjects of the probe.

This was what happened to the innumerable panels of enquiry, (including the visitation panels into Federal

Universities) set up by Babangida in his eight years of thieving and corrupt dictatorship.

The same thing has also happened to the report of the Pius Okigbo panel of enquiry into the accounts of the Central Bank of Nigeria under IBB. This report, which was submitted to Abacha at the time was actively covered up from the Nigerian people in spite of Okigbo's revelation during the presentation ceremony that $12.4 billion of Nigeria's revenue from crude petroleum sales disappeared into the black hole of Babangida's 'dedicated accounts' and was not reflected in the official government accounts kept by the CBN.

The critical challenge which the stubborn persistence and growing virulence of corruption poses to all Nigerians of integrity and conscience is, therefore, how to roll back the escalating phenomenon of corruption in our public life and terminate the culture of impunity that underpins it. Meeting this challenge will involve the mounting of a determined and robust struggle to change the constitutional and legal order and the power configuration in the Nigerian society, such that the vast majority of marginalized Nigerian men and women are empowered to participate freely, actively and maximally in the politics, economy and overall culture of the society. This would mean an end to the 'cash and carry' mode of politics, started with the majority African governments set up in Nigeria in 1952, and carried to its absurd limit during the spurious transition politics of Babangida.

The institutionalization of such an ethos of popular participatory democracy is absolutely essential because the broad masses of our working people, whose interests and well-being are the principal casualties of elite corruption, are the only class of people who can be both objectively and subjectively committed to combating corruption. With this kind of active and committed mass participation, representatives of the working people will be able to monitor closely the behavior of those who are in charge of the state and its treasury and hold them accountable for any crimes against Nigerian humanity, including crimes of corruption and larceny against the wealth of the nation. This necessary expedient of empowering the Nigerian working people vis-a-vis the corrupt and subversive political elite can be facilitated by pursuing the following minimum political agenda of democratic governance:

1. The institutionalization of a multi-party political system in which parties must be genuinely mass-based, national in outlook and exclusively funded by its members' financial contributions, which must be limited to what an ordinary working person can afford. This will safeguard the parties from being high jacked and turned into the political instruments of money bags against the people.

2. The constitutional entrenchment of the principle that the Nigerian people in their respective constituencies have the power to recall at any point in time any elected official who has been found by due process to abuse or betray the people's mandate.

3. The constitutional requirement that only men and women with proven ability and integrity should be appointed to the governing boards of

public institutions, corporations and businesses to ensure that the public resources and assets therein will be safeguarded and enhanced rather than looted and squandered by their official custodians as has hitherto been the case.

4. Freedom of information as an entrenched legal norm to include (a) the requirement of open declaration of assets by all public officers, on entering and leaving office and irrespective of rank or status. Such asset declaration should be available for verification and monitoring by any interested citizen; (b) open and uninhibited access by interested citizens to all documents relating to, or dealing with any aspect of public policy. (This will mean, effectively, the death of all secrecy laws, behind which past and present governments have covered up all manner of crimes against the people).

5. The constitutional entrenchment of freedom of the press as the watchdog of the people's interest, subject only to the limitations imposed by the laws of libel and defamation.

6. The constitutional entrenchment of the principle of independence of the judiciary and the insulation of the appointment and tenure of judges from interference by political decision makers whose conducts might be subjects of adjudication by the courts.

Having discussed the need to curb corruption, our next tasks is how to go about curbing corruption. This is what we shall be doing in the next chapter.

CHAPTER SIX

Measures to Curb Corruption

In this chapter, we shall be looking at proven measures the government can adopt in its resolve to curb corruption. In doing this, we shall be looking at the measures in the Obasanjo and Buhari administrations.

THE OBASANJO AND BUHARI'S STRATEGIES AT CURBING CORRUPTION

In his inaugural presidential address on May 29, 1999 Chief Olusegun Obasanjo vowed to tackle corruption head on. He vowed that "there will be no sacred cows" in his zeal to stamp out deep rooted corruption in the Nigerian society. He even went further to say that "our goal is fight corruption to a standstill." To achieve this, the Obasanjo administration knew there was the need to put in place an effective anti-corruption policy to be taken seriously by the people.

The administration signaled its intention to tackle corruption and increase transparency through a number of initiatives:

1. The Obasanjo administration established the Budget Monitoring and Price Intelligence Unit

(BMPIU) also known as the Due Process Office, headed by Mrs. Oby Ezekwezili, one of the finest minds in Nigeria. This institution was mandated to promote transparency in all government financial transactions and to establish open and competitive tender arrangements for government contracts through the due process mechanism. Through a process of contract award review, oversight, and certification, the government reaped huge savings, estimated at hundreds of millions of dollars. Several contracts that were awarded by spending units that failed to comply with open, competitive bid parameters were cancelled.

2. The administration established the Independent Corrupt Practices and Other Related Offences Commission (ICPC) which was then led by Justice Mustafa Akanbi, one of the best Judges in Nigeria at the time. This Commission recorded great successes in deterring and prosecuting corrupt senior public officers in the country.

3. The privatization process, under the Bureau for Public Enterprises (BPE) headed by Mallam Nasir el-Rufai, was done with high degree of transparency.

4. The administration also forwarded a Public Procurement Bill to the National Assembly. The bill has since been passed into law and the Bureau for Public Procurement (BPP) has institutionalized transparency in the procurement process.

5. One of the landmark achievements of the administration is the establishment of the Economic and Financial Crimes Commission (EFCC) which effectively begun a massive campaign and arrest of persons suspected of fraud. The leadership under the young Mallam Nuhu Ribadu waged an unrelenting war against financial crimes, money laundering and other economic crimes that had created difficulties for Nigeria.

To curb inefficiency, waste, corruption, entrench values in leadership and discourage rent-seeking and other unproductive values, the government introduced the National Economic Empowerment and Development Strategy (NEEDS). The Strategy contains the following measures:

1. Reform, strengthen and modernize institutions whose duty is to foster and enforce compliance. These institutions include: the ICPC, EFCC, NOA, NAFDAC, the Nigerian Police Force, Customs, Immigration, Judiciary, prisons, and the likes.

2. Set up measures to check economic and financial crimes, including the legal provisions for the exposure and punishment of unethical behavior.

3. Adopt a formal code of ethics for all institutions and sectors; publish a code of ethics to engender transparency in the day to day government activities.

4. Institutionalize the process of staff training in ethical behavior and launch a process of leadership by example.

5. To improve transparency and accountability in government's fiscal operations and check unproductive public expenditures by all tiers of government, fiscal responsibility and right to information bills were enacted in 2004. The Fiscal Responsibility Act is required to publish all annually audited accounts by all government agencies and public enterprises within six months of the end of the financial year.

The Buhari administration has equally made its intentions of fighting corruption public. One of the first decisions made by the administration was to set up the Professor Itse Sagay-led Presidential Action Committee Against Corruption. The administration has adopted in the fight against corruption the following:

1. The Presidential Initiative on Continuous Audit (PICA): PICA was set up by President Buhari to strengthen control on public finances through a continuous internal audit process across all ministries, departments and agencies (MDAs), especially in respect to payrolls. Over 53,000 erroneous payroll entries have been identified, and a total of N198 billion has been saved in the process.

2. Budget Reforms: The Ministries, Departments and Agencies (MDAs), against the traditional methods of budget proposals, were to upload their

proposed expenditures on a new budget presentation portal. This system replaced the manual method of budget presentations which is prone to corruption as they are not trackable. The 2017 budget was strengthened against manipulations and alterations by unscrupulous individuals.

3. Expansion of the TSA Coverage: one of the first Executive Orders issued by the Buhari administration was the immediate implementation of the Treasury Single Account (TSA) policy by all MDAs. The policy has resulted in the consolidation of over 20,000 bank accounts and in average monthly savings of N4.7 billion in bank charges.

4. Deployment of the Bank Verification Number (BVN) system for Payroll and Social Investment Programs: The use of BVN to verify Federal Government's payroll entries have led to the detection of over 50,000 "ghost workers" or payroll entries.

5. Replacement of the old Cash-based Accounting System with an up to date Accruals-based system: Accruals-based accounting presents the true financial position of the federal government's assets and liabilities which aids the government's future plans.

6. Enlistment into Open Government Partnership (OGP): in July, 2016 Nigeria became the 70th member of the OGP and has developed a National Action Plan to last between 2017 and 2019.

7. Insistence on Conditionality of Fiscal Support to states: the Fiscal Sustainability Plan (FSP) is a reform program that specifies conditions under which states of the federation can have access to federal government's N510 billion Budget Support Facility (BSF). State governments that fail to implement the FSP action plans according to the conditions will be taken off the BSF with immediate effect.

8. Asset Recovery Reforms: The administration constituted a Presidential Committee on Asset Recovery (PCAR) headed by Vice President, Professor Yemi Osinbajo, to bring together all law enforcement agencies involved in the recovery of assets as well as designation of a dedicated Central Bank account to receive all recovered funds, for efficient management.

9. New Whistle Blowing Policy: The new whistle blowing policy has yielded $160 million and N8 billion in recoveries of stolen public funds.

10. The Federal Ministry of Finance has now established an Efficiency Unit to monitor all ministries, departments and agencies. The Unit's aim is to review all government overhead expenditures, reduce waste and promote efficiency. We shall also vigorously enforce the Public Procurement Act to ensure that due process is followed in government procurements. This has saved the nation untold millions of dollars in revenue.

11. The government also publishes quarterly audits of the hitherto wasteful Nigerian National Petroleum Corporation (NNPC) which was not the case before now.

12. To address the challenge of revenue loss in the unaccounted oil loss, the government has decided to put an end to the opacity in the swapping of crude oil for refined products, which has created avenues for corruption.

All these measures are easy to understand save for the Whistle Blowing Policy which has added a new dimension to the fight against corruption in Nigeria. We shall look at it in details.

THE WHISTLE BLOWING POLICY

In a dramatic dimension to the fight against corruption in Nigeria, never has landmark successes been recorded until the introduction of the Whistle Blowing policy. On the 20th of December, 2016 the Buhari Government of Nigeria introduced what is now known as whistle blowing policy. The policy aims to encourage Nigerians to report financial and other related crimes to relevant authorities. With the government successfully enacting this policy which, to me, is the most ground breaking decision of the Buhari administration so far, the ground is set for an effective anti-corruption war if well implemented. This singular decision by the government should prove to all well-meaning Nigerians that the Buhari administration really means business.

Before we go further we need to know what whistle blowing is. What is Whistle Blowing? This can be regarded as the act of reporting the misconduct of someone (or an official) whose behavior can be inimical to the health of an organization or department. Money laundering, corruption or any other abuse of office can range from between minor issues, to complex, corporate-changing deeds of bad behavior or leadership.

Weeks after the introduction of the policy, the EFCC recorded huge gains. The country home of former NNPC managing director, Andrew Yakubu was raided and huge sums of money were discovered hidden in a safe in a totally obscure building in Southern Kaduna. Days later, properties worth over $37.5 million were discovered in Lagos.

You will agree with me dear readers that these kinds of recoveries especially in such a short period of time could not probably be by accident. Yes, it was not an accident. This level of progress that is now being recorded by the EFCC is surely as a result of some right steps that were taken by the Buhari government. These two incidents are early success stories of this policy.

Even though there have been trickles of successes recorded here and there in the fight against corruption, these latest results are some of the most important victories ever recorded.

The whistle blowing policy is actually much more important to every Nigerian than it initially appears. As a matter of fact, every Nigerian needs to know about this policy. If we really want to combat and win the fight over corruption, we need to have government agencies and none governmental groups popularizing this policy. It is the most ground breaking government decision by the Buhari administration so far.

This policy if well understood by Nigerians would make Nigerians to become participants in the fight against corruption. As the case is right now, I am not sure that most Nigerians are aware of the fact that the whistle blowing policy includes up to 5 PERCENT REWARD OF THE TOTAL AMOUNT OF LOOTS RECOVERED.

There is no way somebody will steal government money of this magnitude without someone else being aware. It is also true that most people who steal are driven by greed, same with their accomplices. In most cases the accomplices are never paid the promised amount, while in other cases they wish to get more than they were promised. It is this despicable human nature that the government and NGOs that are interested in fighting corruption must leverage upon, to spread the word, so that each person that is aware of such evils would be able to speak up.

People must be told that they could become anti-graft agents as citizens. More so, information that could be reported is not limited to stolen funds alone.

Under this policy, citizens are encouraged to report:

1. All forms of mismanagement and misappropriation of public funds and assets

2. Misuse of government properties and vehicles, etc.

3. Financial malpractices of any kind.

4. Any form of fraud especially connected to the common wealth of the nation.

5. Collection or solicitation of bribes.

6. Diversion of payment and revenues.

7. Fraudulent and unapproved payments.

8. Misappropriation of contracts.

9. Kickbacks and over invoicing.

10. Any form of corruption in government or private sectors.

As earlier said, both government and civil societies will have to step up their campaign efforts to inform all Nigerians of their role in fighting corruption. Nigerians must know that building a corruption free society is a collective effort, not just a government responsibility.

We must inform the general public about the definition and the functions of a whistle blower. We must also let the people know that included in this policy is a protection clause. This means that the federal government guarantees and provides security and protection for anybody providing such information. More so the information could be provided incognito that is the person's identity will not be revealed publicly. This tells us that the government has done a lot from their part to carry Nigerians along and involve ordinary Nigerians in building a more chaste society.

Unfortunately, many cultures in Nigeria frowns against whistle blowing. It is thought of as evil or negative to be called a whistle blower. This is due to the fact that the society despises the so called snitch, rat, tattletale, while in Nigeria they are called names like amebo (rumour monger), odale (betrayer), etc. In a culture where this is wide spread, most of the people will be reluctant to participate in this government effort.

However, if we are to build a better future, for our children and posterity, we must stop thinking of the consequences of doing the right thing to ourselves. It is time for us to start to think about the general good and the future of our beloved nation. The most important thing for the whistle blower is to be aware that the information he is providing can be substantiated, that is they are not based on libels, lies and slander.

Even though the government has done a good job by passing this policy into law, I however think they are underestimating how much marketing and promotional work needs to be done for this policy to take root in our nation. This is especially obvious in light of the recent return of former governor James Ibori to Nigeria. The celebration and the atmosphere of merry instead of solemnness that surrounded his return to Nigeria suggests that our people need to be better informed.

I therefore want to use this avenue to thank the people in the Buhari administration who came up with this policy. It is now the turn of every Nigerian to ask what he/she could do to make this campaign a success. If we do, Nigeria will become a better place. A country from where her citizens will not be running anymore, it will be a desirable place for people in the diaspora to come to. Let us all make Nigeria a better place for all.

BUHARI AND INSTITUTIONAL REFORMS IN EFCC AND ICPC

The Buhari administration has since recognized the need for thorough institutional reforms in the two leading anti-corruption agencies, the EFCC and ICPC. The Buhari administration as in its zeal to stamp out corruption became aware that both were presently not working at maximum potential owing to a myriad of challenges, which include overlaps in mandate, gaps in operational legislation and funding, a human capital deficiency, leadership inadequacy and internal corruption.

The need to reposition these institutions became imperative. For instance, currently the ICPC can only begin anti-corruption investigations in response to petitions from the public. The government sought to change that to make it more proactive rather than reactive by revising the ICPC Act to increase the Commission's powers to initiate investigations into cases of corruption.

The new reforms would now include:

- Granting the ICPC the power to commence assets forfeiture proceedings, as is the case in other countries like the US and UK. Illegally acquired properties may then be seized where the suspected owner is a fugitive, disclaims ownership or cannot be located despite diligent efforts.

- Streamlining the jurisdiction of the ICPC by reducing areas of overlap with the EFCC, thus giving each agency areas of primary jurisdictional responsibility.

- Giving the ICPC power to accept material assistance from international institutions and development partners, as well as to access funds from global anti-corruption agencies, which the present ICPC Act prohibits.

Similarly, as part of the EFCC reform, we will focus on:

- Empowering the Commission to presume that a person has illegally enriched themselves where such a person owns, possesses or controls an interest in any property that cannot be justified by present or past emoluments or circumstances.

- Streamlining the jurisdiction of the EFCC to reduce overlap with the ICPC mandate.
- Securing the forfeiture of illegally acquired properties where the suspected owner is a fugitive, disclaims ownership or cannot be located despite diligent efforts.
- Separating the agency for financial intelligence gathering from the EFCC. The Nigerian Financial Intelligence Unit, which operates as an arm of the EFCC, needs to be independent in order to enhance its operational autonomy.

The administration will also need to work with the Legislature to implement all these necessary reforms. It's also critical that these two agencies charged with fighting corruption and financial crimes collaborate closely with development partners for technical assistance, staff training and data sharing.

As international co-operation continues to reduce the number of havens for hiding the proceeds of crime, new havens are emerging. There is the need therefore to enhance the scope of our mutual legal assistance agreements to widen the net the government cast to recover illicit funds and secure the forfeiture of unexplainable assets.

In this regard, the agencies will also need to be more proactive in leveraging the legislations of foreign jurisdictions such as the US Foreign Corrupt Practices Act (US Department of Justice 2015).

BUHARI'S CAMPAIGN FOR ATTITUDINAL CHANGE

On September 8, 2016 President Muhammadu Buhari officially launched the national re-orientation campaign tagged **"Change begins with me"** in Abuja. The campaign is geared towards engendering a holistic attitudinal change in Nigerians, thereby restoring credible value system, spirit of patriotism amongst others. President Buhari said that the long-cherished, time-tested virtues of honesty, integrity have given way to dishonesty, intolerance, indolence and corruption.

In his speech at the launch of the **#ChangeBeginsWithMe** campaign, he said: *"Before you ask where is the change they have promised us, You must ask yourself how far have I changed so far."*

There are insinuations that the launch is a modified package of the defunct War Against Indiscipline, WAI, an anti-social vices program of the military government led by Buhari as Head of State between 1983 and 1985.

Speaking as a Special Guest at the launch of the program initiated by the National Orientation Agency (NOA) under the Federal Ministry of Information and Culture, Buhari charged Nigerians not to see the "change" slogan of his administration only in terms of social and economic reforms but also in the role that individual citizens must play in actualizing it.

According to him, Nigerians can contribute to "change" through the way *"we conduct ourselves, engage our neighbors, friends and generally how we relate with the larger society in a positive and definitive way and manner that promotes our common good and common destiny..."*

122

According to former US President, Barack Obama, *"Change will not come if we wait for some other person or some other time. We are the ones we've been waiting for. We are the change that we seek."*

The word "Change", as I see it, is an aggregation of little steps, tiny deeds here and there, aimed at bringing about a desired change in orientation or circumstance one does not like. What then can be wrong with everyone, putting in their own bit, wherever, however, government and the governed? Or is it a case of another message lost to some ears on account of the source? Or is it that the wave of cynicism has taken over that the power of comprehension is now so diminished?

Whatever the case, I do not think we need anyone to ring the bell before one realizes that change does, in fact, begin with the man in the mirror. It cannot be that difficult to understand. It could be that I am wrong. But I would have thought that 'Change Begins with me' simply means that true change can only come if each one of us plays his or her own part, or does it mean something else? Some insist on making this about who does what first, but I don't see that as the case. It is not about anyone asking you to change before he does.

There are different dimensions to the change. You do your bit, I do mine. That is how we can bring true change about. It is not about looking over the shoulder to see if the other person is on board before doing one's own bit. I have, in fact, found out that, in many instances, it actually takes less energy, especially mental exertion, to do something to change a situation than that spent complaining about it. That, for me, is what this is all about. Why can't change begin with me?

If we all accept to change our behavior; change our attitude and collectively reject corruption the nation will be better for it. My own contribution is in this book you are reading now!

Basis Requirements for the Successful War on Corruption in Nigeria

It is appropriate to emphasize the importance of good and enforceable policies towards controlling corrupt behavior. To achieve this, Robert McNamara, a former World Bank and Ford Foundation president has argued that for any campaign against corruption to be successful in sub-Saharan Africa, certain characteristics should be common in the plans to fight corruption. His suggestions include the following:

1. Requires direct, clear and forceful support of the highest political authority, the president or prime minister. Invariably, no war on corruption can be won without the support of the brass of the political elite;

2. Introduce transparency and accountability in government functions, particularly in all financial transactions;

3. Encourage free press and electronic media to forcefully report to the public on corrupt practices in the society;

4. Organized civil society to address the problem of corruption brought to light by the process of transparency and activity of the media;

5. Introduce into government watch-dog agencies like the anti-corruption bureaus; whistle blowers and the likes which will identify corrupt practices and bring them into public attention;

6. Minimize and simplify government regulations, involving the issuance of licenses, permits and preferential positions, thereby restricting opportunities for rent-seeking by corrupt means;

7. Criminalize all acts of bribery; prohibit the deduction of bribes for tax purposes and erect barriers to prevent transfers of financial gains from corrupt practices to western institutions.

CHAPTER SEVEN

Challenges in the Fight Against Corruption

TO OPPOSE CORRUPTION IN GOVERNMENT IS THE HIGHEST OBLIGATION OF PATRIOTISM.

G. EDWARD GRIFFIN

In this chapter as the title suggests we are going to be talking about the challenges in the fight against corruption, however the gains of victory over corruption are much greater than the challenges. Before I go into the stories of woes that comes out of trying to fight corruption in Nigeria, let me first motivate you by giving you a few statistics about why we must indeed engage in this fight.

When you see the statistics of how much money is being looted from the Nigerian economy, that in itself is enough motivation to pay any price so that this evil is forever uprooted from our national consciousness. In this book I have tried to use as illustration the amount of $200 billion USD that was lost in the last six years, between 2009 and 2015. On one hand it is easier to project and illustrate $200billion USD than $20 trillion USD. I hope that the information I will provide here, will act as an extra motivation for all Nigerians to want to fight corruption to a standstill in our nation.

Let me try to paint a vivid picture of what $200 billion USD would mean to a layman.

- If you were to put $200 billion dollar bills end to end, you could make 20 round trips to the moon!!
- $200 billion dollars could have translated into millions of vaccinations for children, which could have saved the lives of so many kids.
- $200 billion dollars could have become thousands of kilometers of roads constructed.
- $200 billion dollars could have become thousands of schools built.
- $200 billion dollars could have become thousands of hospitals in every town in Nigeria.
- $200 billion dollars could have become 100% water supply in all towns and villages of Nigeria.
- $200 billion dollars could have resolved our electricity problem, giving us 100% supply to every home.

If these statistics are not enough a reason for all Nigerians to arise and fight corruption, then there is no reason being a citizen of Nigeria. Because the future of Nigeria is clearly connected to how well we are able to overcome the mindset of corruption, whatever the cost to each and every one of us.

No doubt, in a complex society like Nigeria, fighting corruption is bound to be a daunting task. Being the major stumbling block to Nigeria's economic growth and development, stamping it out will require a strong leadership that will rise above the mortal tendencies of tribalism, nepotism, partisanship and other parochial interests.

Take a look at some of these challenges: tribalism, ethnicity and nepotism and their potency in the fight against corruption.

Let me share with you some of my experiences in fighting corruption in Nigeria. I have dedicated the last few years to combatting corruption in Nigeria. My journey, though dangerous at times, and uncomfortable and unpleasant for me, has been personally rewarding in ways that I could never have imagined.

As president Buhari himself admitted during an anti-corruption summit in London to mark the Queen's Birthday in May, 2016: *"In the fight against corruption, citizen involvement and demand side activism are key components. Most of our people, especially those in the rural areas who are poor, ignorant and illiterate, do not make the link between corruption and their lack of access to healthcare, education and other facilities, even where they exist. They are too poor, too dependent and too powerless to demand accountability from their State or local governments. We shall therefore encourage the civil society, faith-based groups and community associations to challenge corruption within their communities. In this regard, we shall review our communication strategy towards a more open and transparent government by sharing information, encouraging citizen empower-*

ment and supporting social actions to challenge corrupt practices by public officials at the federal state and local government levels"

The challenges of combating corruption in a resource rich, communal, yet diverse multiethnic societies like Nigeria are multifaceted. In this chapter, I outline some key factors that make the fight against corruption in the country pretty challenging.

ETHNICITY

Nigeria, like many other African societies is multi-ethnic. In truth, all peoples Africans have multiple "identities". For instance, a Nigerian may be a Yoruba, a trained teacher, a Rotarian, a sportsman, a progressive, and a Catholic. And because many of Africa's modern 'tribes' were themselves cobbled together during the colonial period, even ethnicities can be as fluid as the nationalities of the Igbo New York cabbie. While Africans have multiple identities like everyone else, those of negritude and ethnicity have been the most profoundly defining in recent history: the legacy of slavery and colonialism with its critical organized religion.

In an environment 'corrupt behavior' is considered normal it becomes easy to ethnicize corruption. In particular the abuse of public office through egregious conflict of interest and grand corruption on the part of public officials, accompanied by conspicuous consumption on their part, has a disproportionate effect on decisions they make on behalf of the public. This 'corruption', and its assorted manifestations, feed ethnic resentment, compound perceptions of inequality among ethnic groups and lead to policy choices that can undermine economic development in general. Corruption feeds patronage and patronage as a mechanism for redistribution works – it is chaotic, arbitrary and necessarily unjust – but successful as an instrument for managing a population whose sense of ethnic difference from one another form the basic building blocks upon which the leadership exercises governance. So it is not the absolute levels of corruption that complicate matters politically but the extent to which they exacerbate perceptions of economic inequality among different ethnic groups. As a result, ethnicity has become a strong, emotional term among a lot of Nigerians.

Corruption, particularly the egregious conflict of interest on the part of leaders perceived as hailing from one group, and their conspicuous consumption in a flagrant manner, profoundly exacerbates public resentment with regard to graft, even within the context of a growing economy. So, ironically, it is not the corruption in itself that people object to but the fact that it is perpetrated predominantly by an elite from one ethnic group to the exclusion of others, especially theirs. This exclusion can be so persistent that it becomes structural. The resentments and sense of exclusion created by these circumstances often have a more destructive impact than the actual graft itself – a point that is often missed by those who fail to view the issue holistically.

This is important because there are those who argue that corruption as an issue is grossly over-rated and even detrimental to development efforts such as the fight against poverty and underdevelopment. This idea is reassuring to believers in solely technical solutions to economic and political problems – for whom political accountability is seen as destabilizing. Indeed, this is often taken a step further by new-age apologists who argue that good leaders often find themselves surrounded by 'bad people', 'bad advisers'. However compelling, this is nonsense because generally speaking bad leaders surround themselves with bad advisers. The World Bank has recognized and debunked these and other myths of the fight against corruption.

The instrumentalisation of ethics: the assumption that fighting corruption yields economic benefits and this in itself justifies the crusade, has in turn lent ammunition to new-age apologists, especially in the aid industry, who argue that corruption as a problem is overrated because, after all, we have nations where high levels of economic growth and corruption happily co-exist. As we may have noticed in Nigeria, perceptions of ethnic inequality are deepened in heterogeneous societies with a history of patronage. Moreover, the implications of corruption, especially when accompanied by the conspicuous consumption of elites, impact on the political choices both elites and voters make, undermining the quality of democracy and its institutions. At the most basic level this is exemplified by the ambivalent behavior of voters at elections. Voters who rail against the corruption of leaders will happily accept the gifts and handouts of those leaders during elections and their personal patronage after the polls.

MORIBUND CULTURE

The second challenge has to do with moribund culture. In Nigeria we have a convention known as the "big man syndrome". In this case, there is the perception that leaders in responsible government positions are beyond reproach because of their elevated status in society – shapes relationships. There is also a lack of national consciousness. Many people tend to think in groups, such as tribes, instead of as a country. Because of our communal living, an attack on an individual is seen as an attack on the group. Sometimes corruption rewards the group; hence the group is ready to defend the corrupt politician as was the case with former governor James Ibori.

Others believe that corruption is a behavioral pattern that always appears as a consequence of institutional failure. This may be true. But I see corruption as a behavioral pattern built over time because of a lack of foundational, values-based education. Corruption is a human condition, and we have to study how to train up a child in an appropriate way to respect him and respect others and their property. People must be taught to do the right thing.

Legal Issues and Environment

We have a number of legal constraints that undermine the fight against corruption. Only recently were some judges arrested in a sting operation by the Department of State Services (DSS). The judges were caught with huge amounts of hard currencies allegedly taken as bribes from corrupt politicians to hand them favorable judgments.

The judiciary plays critical roles in the fight against corruption. If itself has become corrupt, fighting corruption become a difficult task since those arrested for corrupt charges must be taken to court for prosecution.

Also, the judiciary provides oversight to the enforcement of the law. Those who genuinely feel that their rights are denied or the process was improperly invoked can seek a judicial review of that decision: that is allowed under the system of justice we have. However, it amounts to an unnecessary interference in law enforcement when lawyers engage in legal ingenuity to fish for grounds to get their clients off the hook at all costs, regardless of the true facts. To compound the problem, the judicial process is long-winded and if the court has been misled, cases can be trapped in the convoluted judicial process, frustrating law enforcement and making the anti-corruption war difficult.

Apart from the Judiciary, there are also a number of legislative gaps. There are obvious examples where public officials openly display the proceeds of corruption. We need an unexplained wealth legislative framework to conduct a means test on those public officials.

The National Assembly must cooperate with the executive in this fight if it must be successful. The inability of the Senate to clear the new hardworking EFCC acting chairman, Mr. Ibrahim Magu, as the substantive chairman is an indication of the legislature's determination to frustrate the ongoing anti-corruption war.

The fight against corruption is further undermined by structural weaknesses in political institutions. Political patronage is one of the factors that has, over time, weakened state institutions to such an extent that the line between the bureaucracy and politicians is blurred.

The office of the Auditor-General of the Federation has continued to produce report after report detailing the abject failure of the public service to prevent misuse of public funds. The National Assembly's joint Public Accounts Committee has noted in multiple reports that most of the public servants now spend so much time and energy actively engaged in fraud and corruption that they have little time or incentive to actually deliver services at all. Quite literally, in some departments almost every officer is engaged full-time in attempting to extract public funds out of government accounts.

In Nigeria, there is a new trend whereby institutions of government, independent institutions, are influenced to abuse their own roles just to preserve a few individuals. That erodes public confidence in state institutions. People then resort to informal means of addressing their issues.

The structural changes required to address this situation requires a total re-think of the way that public funds are disbursed and services are delivered in the country. Without a proper diagnosis of the causes of institutional failures, a new set of structural reforms that will subject the bureaucracy to more political control – including proposed reforms to allow MPs to appoint their own departmental heads – could be disastrous. Institutions of government need to be appropriately empowered with the necessary resources and skilled manpower to fight corruption.

Fighting corruption is difficult because of the complex nature of corruption itself. Higher levels of corruption, such as grand corruption, are complex in nature and need specialized skills to uncover. Sometimes the fight against corruption is a double-edged sword. When you uncover certain trends and deal with them, they can develop into more complex forms to tighten their grip.

Indeed, corruption flourishes in secrecy. Those who are aware of corrupt activities going on in their organization rarely report for fear of reprisal. Nigeria's newly launched whistleblower campaign will go a long way to help combat corruption. Later in this book we will discuss the whistleblowing policy in more details. Nigeria also lacks a vibrant media with investigative reporting to utilize the freedom that is guaranteed under the law. The growth of social media has now opened new opportunities for exposing corruption, but little can be done with the information supplied on social media.

Corruption is also transnational making it difficult to address. Cross-border corruption and money laundering are becoming common, yet are rarely curtailed because of jurisdictional and sovereignty issues.

THE POLITICAL ELITE

Moving across Africa, one sees what comprises the national indigenous elite as a creation of the state. It is comprised of former or currently serving state bureaucrats, politicians and members of the security services and their relatives. In its most sophisticated manifestation this elite describes itself as the local private sector but this does not alter the fact that this private sector owes its existence, wealth and social status to its access to and control of the levers of state power and not the 'market' in the traditional sense. The bulk of the Nigerian elite were created in the preceding decades by what came to be described as corruption at the beginning of the 1990s. These elites are the creatures of patronage and conflict of interest, of influence peddling and rent seeking.

Corruption becomes easier to justify on the basis of the need to fund politics, because one ethnic elite feels it needs the fire to fight the fire of the corruptly accumulated financial resources of the previous elite and because, put quite simply, it has worked for those who have come before.

These political contradictions are where the fight against corruption has so far reached. It is the metaphorical glass ceiling. The question of who pays for elections in Nigeria remains unanswered and not properly addressed. In the meantime it is often corruption that pays for the most effective political campaigns. In some countries the possibility of public financing of political parties has been considered but not seriously. In truth, political financing remains occasionally problematic even in mature democracies. In Nigeria it is where the fight against corruption has reached.

The fight against corruption is not an easy one and no one should think it will be because it has become systemic and endemic. For a very long time, our economy and national life have been sustained by corruption. Our politics was built around corruption and our social language is corruption. There are many explanations about how we got to this path but the truth is that successive governments have paid lips service to addressing the challenges of corruption. It appears the citizens have become accustomed to its prevalence and our systems are dependent on it. We fail in most instances to see the real challenges that corruption poses for us as country.

There is no doubt in anybody's mind that the deep economic challenges we now face as a country were exacerbated or even triggered, in some instances, by corruption. Rather than these realities to be a deterrent, events continue to show the uncommon tolerance for corruption in Nigeria, often displayed in our shameless celebration of felons and obeisance to questionable wealth.

The Buhari government has left no one in doubt that it is committed to fighting corruption. While there are concerns about the method and effectiveness of its strategy, these concerns do not detract from the fact that these current efforts are unprecedented. The danger, however, is that we may apply dedication and energy to fighting corruption without necessarily achieving the desired results. It is imperative that government should urgently adopt and release its holistic anti-corruption strategy. This strategy has been a draft for too long and needs to now become a living document that provides clear road maps, measurable expectations and a viable framework for fighting corruption.

Every arm of government must be equally committed to this effort. The National Assembly and judiciary must own this process as much as the executive. Government must also be keenly aware that corruption would fight back and will look for every means to discredit this process. Against this reality, government must ensure that the fight against corruption must be within the law. It is also necessary that key government officials, who are implicated or entangled in allegations of corruption, should be investigated in manner that elicits confidence and trust in the process. Any public perception that government is shielding individuals from investigation is a major blow to the anti-corruption effort.

People must buy into this anti-corruption effort for it to succeed and the greatest tool for public enlightenment is leadership by example. Citizens must perceive government to be fair, objective, credible and incorruptible. This is a tough call but through creative communication, consultation and the resolute enforcement of rules, government can come off as sincere. Every Nigerian is a key partner in the fight against corruption. However, the civil society, trade union, professional organizations and faith based groups have a special role of supporting government, educating citizens and being watchdogs. It is in the best interest of Nigerians for us to live in a country where corruption is an exception and not the general rule.

CHAPTER EIGHT

Surmounting the Challenges of Fighting Corruption

With the understanding that corruption poses a big threat to the Nigerian economy, we shall be arguing in this chapter how to survive the challenges involved in curbing corruption. The chapter will be recommending practical approaches, using the mass media and other agents of influence, in surmounting this scourge.

The biggest challenge to fighting corruption in Nigeria is to get the whole Nigerian population motivated enough to join in the fight. As the title of this book suggests, one of the reasons why I called this book how the Nigerian economy can overtake America's economy, is to paint a vivid picture of the enormous potential the country possesses. It is my hope and expectations that if ordinary Nigerians would know that their country could be as great as America that could be enough motivation to want to do anything possible to see that becomes a reality. Indeed the only thing necessary to be done is to join the campaign of the populace against the cancer of corruption.

Nevertheless, in this chapter of the book, I have decided to again try to find an additional factor of motivation to every Nigerian on why they must begin to act actively and aggressively against our biggest enemy which is corruption. The example I want to use as motivation for my fellow Nigerians before I fully expand on the subject of this chapter is that of a country which is very familiar to most Nigerians. I am talking of the nation of Dubai.

Most Nigerians now talk about Dubai as an example of the wonder country their leaders have failed to build for them. Indeed, with the help of every Nigerian citizens fighting against corruption, we can actually build many Dubai in Nigeria.

Let me however remind you that we are only talking of the $200 billion USD that was lost only in the oil sector of Nigeria between the years 2009 - 2015

Let's paint another picture. Dubai has become one of the wonders of the 21st century and the wonder of Dubai itself is called the Burj Khalifa building. It is the tallest building in the world measuring 2, 723ft. For comparisons sake, it was built for 1.5 billion USD.

If we are now saying, that in 6 years we lost 200 billion USD, with that amount of money judiciously used, every state capital in Nigeria will have their own Burj Khalifa building. That on its own would make Nigeria a tourist attraction, more than Dubai and maybe more than the United States of America. Nigeria only has 36 states. After constructing this massive structure in every state, we will still have enough money to build over 70 more of such structures.

What I am trying to say is that the harm corruption is doing to our country is so bad that I advocate for every Nigerian, at home and abroad, to join the crusade against this deadly practice in our nation. We have to fight it with everything we have.

PUBLIC PARTICIPATION IN THE ANTI - CORRUPTION WAR

Governance, as defined by the World Bank, is *"(the) exercise of economic, political and administrative authority to manage a country's affairs at all levels. It comprises the mechanisms, processes and institutions through which citizens and groups articulate their interests, exercise their legal rights, meet their obligations and mediate their differences. Governance encompasses the state, but transcends the state by including the private sector and civil society organizations."*

One good way to ensure public participation in the anti-corruption war is to make governance accountable, participatory and transparent. This will ensure that political, social and economic priorities are based on broad consensus in society and that the voices of the poorest and the most vulnerable are included not only in the allocation of resources but also in the decision making process. One of the principal causes of "bad governance" is the existence of corruption. Conversely, one of the core foundations of good governance is accountability - the obligation to render an account for a responsibility conferred. In government, accountability is a process that subjects a form of control over departments and agencies, causing them to give a general accounting for their actions - an essential concept in democratic public

143

administration. Consequently, there is a need for more effective and efficient public service institutions that are designed to maximize the use of public resources.

ROLE OF THE MEDIA IN THE WAR AGAINST CORRUPTION

How effective is the media in checking corruption in Nigeria? According to the BBC Media Action, there is good evidence to support the role of media in acting as a check on corruption. The BBC Media Action found out that the press is essential to checking abuse of executive power. They also suggest that the media continue to be at least as relevant to curbing corruption as many of the anti-corruption initiatives different development actors have supported in recent years. The question therefore is: How effective is the media in checking corruption?

In a study commissioned by the United Kingdom's Department for International Development (DFID) in 2015, it concluded that *"direct anti-corruption inter-ventions, which were especially prominent during the 1990s and 2000s, including efforts such as anti-corruption authorities, national anti-corruption strategies, and national anti-corruption legislation... were found to be ineffective in combating corruption"*[7]. So what went wrong?

Any attempt at fighting corruption without effective media is bound to fail. As the same DFID-commissioned study found that the media has a clear effect in reducing corruption, alongside measures such as improving procurement. The same study observed: *"There is a small body of evidence relying primarily on observational studies making use of statistical analyses.*

This evidence consistently indicates [that] freedom of the press can reduce corruption and that the media plays a role in the effectiveness of other social accountability mechanisms". The same paper still concluded that when media freedom is curtailed, corruption tends to rise, finding evidence of *"restrictions to press freedom leading to higher levels of corruption in a sample of 51 developed and developing countries".*

In a study carried out by the World Bank[8] on the evidence around the political impact of transparency efforts (much of it focused on the role of the media) concluded that *"information from trustworthy sources can increase political participation and allow voters to punish badly-performing politicians at the polls, [but] more research is necessary to develop an understanding of both the long-term effects of information provision as well as the general equilibrium effects taking into account public officials', politicians', and parties' responses."*

The right to know is inextricably linked to accountability. Informed appraisal of government by the public, press and parliament is a difficult, even impossible, task if government activities and decision-making processes are obscured from public scrutiny.

Legislation is often required. Hence, many reformers have moved to institute the concept of freedom of information (FOI) legislation. Not only can FOI legislation establish a right of review by an ombudsman, but it can also establish regulations that legislate compliance. It helps reverse the presumption of secrecy. Citizens are given the legal right of access to official documents without having to first prove special interest, and the burden of justifying non-disclosure falls on the government. Of course there is allowance for preventing disclosure of documents that contain information that would comprise national security or the public interest if revealed, such as criminal investigations, budget proposals and sensitive economic information.

FOI is enhanced by a free press, which ranks alongside an independent judiciary as one of the twin powers that serve as a powerful counterforce to malfeasance. Unlike judges, public prosecutors and attorneys-general, the public-not politicians-sustains the privately owned media. Regardless of ownership, the media should be, and can be, free of political patronage.

The degree to which the media is independent is the degree to which it can perform effectively as a public watchdog. Through the responsible judgment of editors and journalists, a culture of a free press develops. This culture is an important guarantor of its ability to operate as a watchdog. Just as the legislature should keep the executive branch under daily scrutiny, the media should diligently monitor both the legislature and the executive to determine if they are engaged in dishonest activity. Politicians and civil servants may be more tempted to abuse their positions for private gain when they are confident they run no risk of public exposure and humiliation through the media. Even today, many countries censor the press and jail journalists.

Laws declaring freedom of expression require support and enforcement from the courts. An independent judiciary is the handmaiden of a free press. A prerequisite for building a free press, therefore, is a legal system that is independent of political influence and that has firm constitutional support. Independence of the media is a complex concept. In general terms, it focuses on the philosophy that journalists should be free of interference from authorities in the responsible pursuit and practice of their profession. In reality, media owners may intervene, daily, in the operations of the journalists in their employ. In many countries, the government is the largest owner of the media, which can undermine its independence. When this happens, efforts should be made to strengthen the media's independence, possibly through privatization or diversification. The latter may increase competition; stimulating a wider range of perspectives on public policy issues and providing a check on the political power of media magnates.

In numerous countries, laws uphold the notion of a free press and include constraints in the form of "reasonable limits" on grounds of national security or individual privacy. There may be instances when national security demands limits on the media, for example to control hate literature or curb racial and ethnic tensions. Appropriate legislation can guard against the abuse of such discretion.

THE ROLE OF THE JUDICIARY IN THE FIGHT AGAINST CORRUPTION

The Judiciary is one institution that is critical to our ability to successfully combat corruption. Yet our Judiciary itself is perceived to be corrupt. As in other areas, it's a difficult allegation to prove. From their pronouncements, it's clear that the leadership of the Judiciary is aware of this general perception. This cannot be swept under the carpet, especially given the odious nature of many decisions from the Bench. These include granting perpetual injunctions, restraining the police and anti-corruption agencies from investigating, arresting or prosecuting high-profile politicians and the other examples we cited in Ibori and Alamiesiegha.

As we all know, like many other democracies in the world, there are three organs of government, the Legislative arm represented by the National Assembly ; the Executive, represented by the President and his ministers; and the Judiciary represented by the Courts. As we grew up knowing, "the Judiciary is the last hope of the common man." The question has always been, what if the Judiciary itself becomes corrupt?

According to Sections 6 and 272 of the 1999 Constitution, the main function of the judiciary and several other courts are clearly spelt out. The judiciary interprets the Constitution. It also serves as watch dog of the Constitution. Therefore, since the ball of anti-corruption ends on the desk of the judiciary, this organ of government becomes crucial in the war against corruption.

There are several individuals facing trials for corruption and related offences in the country. Many of them have been discharged for want of evidence or other technical grounds. Among this category of people are former Governors, ministers, permanent secretaries and other high profile accused persons.

The Judiciary has a difficult task of tackling corruption according to the laws of the land. They cannot manufacture laws on their own. The days when we had the likes of Justice Kayode Esho, who we can classify as one of the incorruptible judges are far gone. Many of the judges we have now, with due respect to those working hard to sanitize the Judiciary of corruption, are corrupt.

The case of Chief James Ibori, former governor of Delta state still came to my mind. As a matter of fact, he was not found guilty by any Nigerian court until a Royal Court in London found him guilty of looting his state resources sentencing him to 13 years imprisonment. To me, this is a big indictment on the Nigerian Judiciary. Yet, our judges continued as though nothing bad happened.

I do not want to believe that there are not enough laws to prosecute corrupt people in Nigeria. What we seem not to have are fearless individuals who can be bold enough to call a spade by its name instead of calling it a shovel.

To fight corruption we have several institutions: Code of Conduct Bureau, Public Complaints Commission, the Attorney-General of the Federation's Office, Office of the Inspector General of Police, Office of the Auditor-General of the Federation and the likes are institutions created to fight corruption. With all these in place, there seem to be no bold and selfless persons to occupy these offices.

One thing we must do away with in Nigeria is this idea of **"It is better for a criminal to go free than for an innocent man to be punished."** This innocent until proven guilty British tradition has led many to escape prosecution. May be we need to modernize this policy to fit our Nigerian and African reality to ensure that criminals don't take advantage of the system and go scot free.

To be fair, the Judiciary through the National Judicial Council (NJC) has been able to do little fighting corruption within its fold. The bribery involving the Akwa-Ibom Election Petition Tribunal raised by an All

Nigerian Peoples Party (ANPP) governorship candidate against some judicial officers in 2003 were handled effectively by the Council in my opinion. But are all these enough?

Why has the Judiciary been handicapped in the fight against corruption? It is a known fact that a society can only survive in the attainment of justice through its legal system. The appointment of judges in Nigeria needs to be revisited. It is fast looking to me like one needs political affiliations to be appointed a judge in Nigeria. The recent drama involving the arrest of some judges in Rivers state attest to this fact. A situation where huge amounts of money were found in some Judge's possession is worrisome. The question was how were they appointed in the first instance? Was there a thorough security or background check on these individuals before their appointments done in the first instance? I doubt these!

When a Judge earns less than a member of a state House of Assembly member he may not command respect. More often than not, there is no security for these judges after their retirements. Many will almost live lonely and poor lives after they retire from the service. Things like these make them vulnerable to corruption in a society that places much value on material wealth!

The moral values in the Nigerian society need to be looked into. The Judiciary would lose the war on corruption, and frustratingly too, because a society that does not have a strong moral foundation will more often than not produce leaders who lack character and values. These are what fuels corruption!

WHAT IS TO BE DONE?

The issue of corruption has come to center stage of political and economic discourses in Nigeria. The economic consequences of pervasive corruption and recent trends toward democratization have increased the pressure in public officeholders to adhere to standards of accountability and transparency in the performance of their duties.

Our argument in this book does not suggest that the solutions to corruption are easy, neither does it suggest that any country has found an ideal model to limit corruption, nor that such a model even exists. It does argue, however, that while each country or region is unique in its history and culture, political system and stage of economic and social development, similarities in national integrity systems do exist and lessons learned are often transferable.

A national integrity system comprises a number of principle elements.

Those suggested in this book - public awareness and participation, accountability and transparency in the judicial system and the media - are some of the pillars of a national integrity system and the foundations of sustainable development. However, alone, any one of these elements will have only limited impact in the fight against corruption. Ethical codes or new procurement rules, for example, will have little effect unless they are implemented and enforced by independent agencies. An ombudsman office, financial management and auditing systems, and anti-corruption agencies are examples of watchdog authorities that can monitor compliance with the rule of law.

Similarly, reform strategies depend on the active support and vigilance of civil society and the media. A responsible media can be enlisted to raise public awareness of the harmful repercussions of corruption and of citizens' rights to expect ethical conduct from their government. The elements of a national integrity system are mutually reinforcing.

All of these elements do not have to be instituted or strengthened simultaneously. The schematic to initiate and manage a national integrity system determines the success or failure of reform efforts. Each country must define the most strategic elements for change in order to maximize existing opportunities while providing critical support to areas that, left unattended, could undermine the reform program. Moreover, a few successful and substantial measures are more effective than grand, marginally successful programs at demonstrating to the public government leaders' and representatives' willingness to fight corruption seriously.

In Nigeria, regardless of our multiethnic nature, promotion of a national integrity system and the fight against corruption must be as politically inclusive and citizen-friendly as possible. This requires the following:

1. A committed, non-partisan political leadership that shows its commitment by willingly submitting to a comprehensive monitoring of assets, incomes, liabilities and lifestyles;

2. Public involvement and participation in the reform process, with proposed changes debated widely to generate a sense of ownership among the public and to reinforce the values embodied in reform;

3. Participation by civil service unions and other employee groups;

4. Involvement of professional groups and community and religious leaders.

Performance targets and monitoring systems must be in place to measure progress toward reduced corruption. To be effective, results-oriented management must create incentive structures and an enabling environment to encourage achievement of civil service reform targets and quality results. These results should be disseminated to the public at large. Sharing information with civil society represents a significant step in ensuring transparency and accountability in government.

THE GOVERNMENT NEEDS OUR SUPPORT

High-level corruption mostly involves politicians, hence fighting corruption requires genuine and consistent political support at the highest level in order to succeed. Fighting corruption is a politically-charged battle, which is won through genuine political will which the Buhari administration has taken the lead. In order to have trust in the political will, the political leadership must lead by example.

The fight against corruption cannot be successful without Non-Governmental Organizations and groups. We need an independent and vibrant civil society, media and Labor Union to provide unbiased criticism to corrupt activities. We need a group of civic-minded citizens who must rise-up and care enough to do something about the prevalence of corruption.

The fight against corruption must never be thought of as one-man show. The Buhari administration needs our support and encouragement. Corruption does fight back. In ideal societies, you would expect that individuals who are the subject of corruption scandals will own-up and submit themselves with the opportunity provided by the whistle blowing policy. But in Nigeria, we are facing ingrained resistance to accountability, which is adding another layer to the challenge.

As a result, fighting corruption in an environment like Nigeria, needs not just consummate professionalism, but courage. There are two elements of that courage. First, we need courage to pay the price. Many people fear retribution, be it the fear of losing their job, perks and privileges or being alone or losing their lives. In a country where the job market is limited, the government is the major employer and contractor. Those who control the systems may be part of a group: you try to attack a group and you become their enemy. Second, we need to be clean: the corrupt cannot fight corruption. They will dig your grave and hunt you to your tomb. If you have no skeletons in your own closet, you will not fear anybody.

From my experience, when you raise the anti-corruption temperature in a country like ours, it starts to make people uncomfortable. If the temperature is too hot and you get a bit too close to the sun, you get burnt. Nigeria needs more men and women of courage to stand up for their country, even at a personal cost. Honesty can be costly, but you have to stay the course.

CHAPTER NINE

Nigeria's New Whistle Blowing Policy

As I had said earlier in this book, before Nigeria can attain her potential of becoming one of the greatest countries in the world and especially if we want to attain the dream of Nigeria's economy overtaking America's economy, one major prerequisite is that there must be a wider citizen participation in the fight against corruption. Luckily for all of us, this new administration of Muhammudu Buhari, seems to have gotten the message at last by enacting the whistle blowing policy.

In this chapter I am sharing with you the article that I wrote at the time this policy took effect in the nation. We will use this whole chapter to discuss this topic in more details. Let's go!

Early in 2017, the Nigerian news media world was engulfed in shocking revelations after the discoveries by the Economic and Financial Crimes Commission (EFCC).

WOE TO HIM WHO BUILDS HIS HOUSE BY
UNJUST GAIN, SETTING HIS NEST ON HIGH
TO ESCAPE THE CLUTCHES OF RUIN!

HABAKKUK 2:9

The most mind blowing of these discoveries was the news that the amount of $9.8 million US dollars and another 75,000 British pounds which was connected to the former group managing director of the Nigerian National Petroleum Corporation (NNPC) Mr. Andrew Yakubu was recovered after a raid was carried out at one of his houses in Kaduna State. The money was hidden in such a way that it could not be discovered by someone who did not have prior knowledge. The perpetrators had gone to the extent of even providing a fire proof protection for the safe.

A few days later, the EFCC again, recorded another ground breaking discovery, when they found a house in banana island Lagos, which is worth a whopping $37.5 million US dollars. For the Nigerian mind to fully grasp what that means in Nigeria currency, a $37.5 Million US dollar house will equal, 11.25 billion Naira.

This is at a time when Nigerians are gnashing their teeth in the pain of poverty, sky rocketing prices, inflation, unemployment, etc. As a matter of fact, more than half the population of Nigerians are said to be living on less than $2 US dollars a day. Meanwhile one former government official owns a house that costs billions of Naira. The irony is that nobody lives in this house. It is just a way of stashing away money in real estate.

This property was acquired by the former minister of petroleum, Mrs. Diezani Alison-Madueke. Last year another building was ceased from this same former minister costing $18 million US dollars in the Asokoro area of Abuja.

> HER OFFICIALS WITHIN HER ARE LIKE WOLVES TEARING THEIR PREY; THEY SHED BLOOD AND KILL PEOPLE TO MAKE UNJUST GAIN.
>
> EZEKIEL 22:27

Why am I going into all these stories and history of recoveries? This is all because I wish to point the attention of Nigerians to what they have missed in the barrage of news that daily hits the Nigerian airwaves.

COULD THIS BE COINCIDENCE?

You will agree with me dear readers that these kind of recoveries especially in such a short period of time could not probably be by accident. Yes, it was not an accident. This level of progress that is now being recorded by the EFCC is surely as a result of some right steps that were taken by the Nigerian government.

> THERE IS NO COMPROMISE WHEN IT COMES TO CORRUPTION. YOU HAVE TO FIGHT IT.
>
> A. K. ANTHONY.

In early 2017, the federal government of Nigeria, successfully enacted a whistle blowing policy, which to me is the most ground breaking decision of the Buhari administration so far. This singular decision by the government should prove to all well-meaning Nigerians that the Buhari administration really means business.

One of the platforms on which the APC party and Buhari campaigned upon to win the general presidential election from the Goodluck Jonathan administration, was to fight corruption to a standstill. Even though there have been trickles of successes recorded here and there in the fight against corruption, these latest results are some of the most important victories ever recorded.

THEY HAVE SUNK DEEP INTO CORRUPTION, AS IN THE DAYS OF GIBEAH. GOD WILL REMEMBER THEIR WICKEDNESS AND PUNISH THEM FOR THEIR SINS.

HOSEA 9:9

The whistle blowing policy is actually much more important to every Nigerian than it initially appears. As a matter of fact, every Nigerian needs to know about this policy. If we really want to combat and win the fight over corruption, we need to have government agencies and none governmental groups popularizing this policy. It is the most ground breaking government decision by the Buhari administration so far.

5 PERCENT REWARD

This policy if well understood by Nigerians would make Nigerians to become participants in the fight against corruption. As the case is right now, I am not sure that most Nigerians are aware of the fact that the whistle blowing policy includes up to 5 PERCENT REWARD OF THE TOTAL AMOUNT OF LOOTS RECOVERED.

There is no way somebody will steal government money of this magnitude without someone else being aware. It is also true that most people who steal are driven by greed, same with the accomplices. In most cases the accomplices are never paid the promised amount, while in other cases they wish to get more than they were promised. It is this despicable human nature that the government and NGOs that are interested in fighting corruption must leverage upon, to spread the word, so that each person that is aware of such evils would be able to speak up.

WHERE DO THE EVILS LIKE CORRUPTION ARISE FROM? IT COMES FROM THE NEVER-ENDING GREED. THE FIGHT FOR CORRUPTION-FREE ETHICAL SOCIETY WILL HAVE TO BE FOUGHT AGAINST THIS GREED AND REPLACE IT WITH 'WHAT CAN I GIVE' SPIRIT.

A. P. J. ABDUL KALAM

People must be told that they could become anti-graft agents as citizens. More so, the information that could be reported is not limited to stolen funds alone.

From the flying news: whistle blowers are the latest billionaires in town:

Andrew Yakubu whistle blower got N250,000,000 instantly from FG (Nigeria Federal Government). We (EFCC) have been receiving more whistle blowing information since Andrew Yakubu raid, we will attend to all and we are aware of those hurriedly relocating their loots but unfortunately those helping them in the relocations are updating us. Blow a whistle today and receive an instant 5% of the loots from FG – EFCC.

IN YOU ARE PEOPLE WHO ACCEPT BRIBES TO SHED BLOOD; YOU TAKE INTEREST AND MAKE A PROFIT FROM THE POOR. YOU EXTORT UNJUST GAIN FROM YOUR NEIGH-BORS. AND YOU HAVE FORGOTTEN ME, DECLARES THE SOVEREIGN LORD.

EZEKIEL 22:12

CITIZENS ARE ENCOURAGED TO REPORT

All forms of mismanagement and misappropriation of public funds and assets

1. Misuse of government properties and vehicles, etc.

2. Financial malpractices of any kind.

3. Any form of fraud especially connected to the common wealth of the nation.

4. Collection or solicitation of bribes.

5. Diversion of payment and revenues.

6. Fraudulent and unapproved payments.

7. Misappropriation of contracts.

8. Kickbacks and over invoicing.

9. Any form of corruption in government or private sectors.

As earlier said, both government and civil societies will have to step up their campaign efforts to inform all Nigerians of their role in fighting corruption. Nigerians must know that building a corruption free society is a collective effort, not just a government responsibility.

We must inform the general public about the definition and the functions of a whistle blower. We must also let the people know that included in this policy is a protection clause. Meaning that the federal government guarantees and provides security and protection for anybody providing such information. More so the information could be provided incognito, which is the person's identity will not be revealed publicly. This tells us that the government has done a lot from their part to carry Nigerians along and involve ordinary Nigerians in building a more chaste society.

LIKE A PARTRIDGE THAT HATCHES EGGS IT DID NOT LAY ARE THOSE WHO GAIN RICHES BY UNJUST MEANS. WHEN THEIR LIVES ARE HALF GONE, THEIR RICHES WILL DESERT THEM, AND IN THE END THEY WILL PROVE TO BE FOOLS.

JEREMIAH 17:11

So Who is a Whistle Blower?

Unfortunately, because of our cultural mindset, most of our people will think it evil or negative to be called a whistle blower. This is due to the fact that the society despises the so called snitch, rat, tattletale, while in Nigeria they are called names like amebo, odale, etc. In a culture where this is wide spread, most of the people will be reluctant to participate in this government effort.

> WOE TO THOSE WHO CALL EVIL GOOD AND GOOD EVIL, WHO PUT DARKNESS FOR LIGHT AND LIGHT FOR DARKNESS, WHO PUT BITTER FOR SWEET AND SWEET FOR BITTER!
>
> ISAIAH 5:20

However, if we are to build a better future, for our children and posterity, we must stop thinking of the consequences of doing the right thing to ourselves. It is time for us to start to think about the general good and the future of our beloved nation. The most important thing for the whistle blower is to be aware that the information he is providing can be substantiated, that is they are not based on libels, lies and slander.

A whistle blower could be defined as someone who is driven by the greater good of the country and hence voluntarily discloses information at his disposal in good faith and discretion. A whistle blower informs the authorities about a possible misconduct or violation of the law that has occurred, is ongoing or about to take place.

> THE FIRST SIGN OF CORRUPTION IN A SOCIETY THAT IS STILL ALIVE IS THAT THE END JUSTIFIES THE MEANS.
>
> GEORGES BERNANOS

Even though the government has done a good job by enacting this policy, I however think they are underestimating how much marketing and promotional work needs to be done for this policy to take root in our nation. This is especially obvious in light of the recent return of former governor James Ibori to Nigeria. The celebration and the atmosphere of merry instead of solemnness that surrounded his return to Nigeria suggests that our people need to be better informed.

> I WILL SURELY STRIKE MY HANDS TOGETHER AT THE UNJUST GAIN YOU HAVE MADE AND AT THE BLOOD YOU HAVE SHED IN YOUR MIDST.
>
> EZEKIEL 22:13

THE NEED FOR MASS PROMOTION

In a country where people are rejoicing that a convicted government official has given them a little bit of the goodies he stole instead of reporting to the appropriate government agencies, shows that something must be done to correct the people's value system. It is obvious that the people are not aware that the goodies and spoils that are being distributed to them by these corrupt individuals is a part of the money that is meant for them, the masses. In a situation where a corrupt politician dolls out a million US dollars, be sure that he has stolen about a billion US dollars from the people. He has only given them one percent of what is meant for them. Yet, my people gullibly rejoice and go as far as fighting to protect these corrupt officials.

A JUST KING GIVES STABILITY TO HIS NATION, BUT ONE WHO DEMANDS BRIBES DESTROYS IT.

PROVERBS 29:4

Another fact that confirms the need for more propagation of anti-graft policies in the country was recorded a few years back when another governor was arrested overseas, yet managed to escape and run back to the country by disguising as a woman. On his arrival, his people were celebrating him while attacking the government. Blaming the government for his so called plight while totally ignoring the abuse of office and the corruption charges he faced. To his people he is seen as a hero because they had managed to receive some crumbs from his enormous spoils. Unfortunately, these people are celebrating and fighting for the rights of the official who has led them to the abyssal state they are in right now.

It is like a man who stole all your belongings that are worth a million US dollars and then comes back to you to act as the philanthropist while giving you back $10 US dollars. Using $10 US Dollars of your one million dollars to give you a feast. The uninformed populace meanwhile rejoice and celebrate because they had a feast. Some of them even go to the extent of risking their lives to protect the corrupt officials. This is the picture of what is happening in Nigeria right now. This is the more reason why NGOs and civil societies should take over this campaign to sanitize and get our people better informed.

As I write right now, there is an ongoing drama where a federal senator is being charged and looked for in America as a criminal, meanwhile he is a senator here at home in Nigeria. The reason why he was elected as a senator is because he has been splashing some of his money on the electorate and the people keep on supporting him.

I am aware that there is an Online portal and telephone number that could be used by these whistle blowers to submit their information through email or by telephone, yet not too many people know this information. That is why I believe that such information must be propagated and made readily available to all Nigerians wherever they are.

Government Contact Information For Whistle Blowers:
Tel: 09098067946
Website: www.finance.gov.ng
Email: Whistle@finance.gov.ng

It is my belief that if this policy of whistle blowing is well propagated and promoted to the general public, every Nigerian will stand to gain and our country will be the better for it.

ADVANTAGES OF WHISTLE BLOWING

ANYONE WHO HAS BEEN STEALING MUST STEAL NO LONGER, BUT MUST WORK, DOING SOMETHING USEFUL WITH THEIR OWN HANDS, THAT THEY MAY HAVE SOMETHING TO SHARE WITH THOSE IN NEED.

EPHESIANS 4:28

What are some of the advantages these policies could bring to the country?

1. It would help bring in some much needed cash that could be used to solve some of the myriad list of problems.

2. The recovery of stolen cash will help improve our inflation rate.

3. Since a lot of these money are in foreign currencies, this could help the exchange rate of the naira.

4. Some of the money could be used to build some infrastructure and amenities needed for economic recovery.

5. Pensions could be paid to the senior citizens and pensioners who have been wallowing in poverty and lack.

6. More schools and universities could be built.

7. We could limit the number of strikes by civil servants, teachers, petroleum workers, etc by paying their salaries.

8. More world class hospitals, roads, etc, could be built.

9. The supply and provision of electricity and water could be improved.

10. The level of crime and corruption in the country generally will decrease.

11. This fight against corruption would also help improve the level of public confidence in government and in the country in general, thereby leading to greater inflow of investment into the country.

12. It would encourage transparency and accountability by public officials.

Do You Know Dr. George Uboh?

Not too many people are aware of who Doctor George Uboh is, but the fact is that we need thousands more of Dr. Uboh in Nigeria. Dr. Uboh is the foremost whistle blower in Nigeria. He has faced victimization, illegal detentions, physical, cyber and spiritual threats, just for blowing whistle on some of the Nigerian corrupt officials.

Dr. Uboh has vowed to lay down his life if necessary, in his effort to expose corrupt practices in our country. Many Nigerians should know that there are people like Dr. Uboh already doing the job. They should also know that no amount of black magic or spiritual attacks have been able to stop him because nothing defeats the truth. As long as you are sure that your conviction is based on the truth, the truth will always fight for you.

One of the most important aspects of this policy as I have mentioned earlier is that it protects the whistle blowers. The government at their own cost have taken it upon themselves to provide security and protection to anybody that will submit relevant information against grafts and corruption in our country.

It should also be noted that those who give evil and mischievous information about innocent people will be reprimanded. This is important so that individuals will not turn this policy into a weapon of personal and political vendetta.

THE LORD ALMIGHTY DECLARES, "I WILL SEND IT OUT, AND IT WILL ENTER THE HOUSE OF THE THIEF AND THE HOUSE OF ANYONE WHO SWEARS FALSELY BY MY NAME. IT WILL REMAIN IN THAT HOUSE AND DESTROY IT COMPLETELY, BOTH ITS TIMBERS AND ITS STONES.

ZECHARIAH 5:4

People like Dr. Uboh are convinced that Nigeria could reduce corruption by 90%, but that is only dependent on how widespread this campaign goes to the grassroots. I therefore want to use this opportunity to appeal to Nigerians all and sundry, to join this campaign. This is not about a political party, this is one of the most important government policies in our country today. We should all join it to make Nigeria better.

It is only thanks to this policy that Andrew Yakubu's largesse were discovered despite all the protection that was put in place. Somebody who knew about it blew the whistle. The same applied to the discovery of the 11 billion naira house belonging to former petroleum Minister Diezani Madueke.

As you all could see, the latest successes of our anti-graft agency (EFCC) is mainly thanks to the efforts of ordinary citizens in submitting relevant information to the right agencies.

THEREFORE, UNTIL THE DAY I DIE, I AM
GOING TO DO WHAT I CAN, REGARDLESS
OF THE COST TO ME, TO TRY TO STOP THIS
AWFUL CORRUPTION THAT IS DESTROYING
OUR BELOVED DEMOCRACY.

JOHN JAY HOOKER

I therefore want to use this avenue to thank the people in the Buhari administration who came up with this policy. It is now the turn of every Nigerian to ask what he or she could do to make this campaign a success. If we do, Nigeria will become a better place. A country from where her citizens will not be running anymore. It will be a desirable place for people in the diaspora to come to. Let us all make Nigeria a better place for all.

CHAPTER TEN

Church and Nation-Building

In this chapter we shall be taking a look at the role of the Church in Nation-Building, specifically in the fight against corruption. What should the church be doing? What are we doing? What did we not do? How can we correct our wrongs?

In writing this Chapter, I debated between using the "Faith community", "Church as an Institution" or "Religious bodies" and a replacement for "Church and Nation-Building". First of all, let us understand what we mean by nation building.

WHAT IS NATION-BUILDING?

Nation building as a concept became prominent in the 1960s and early 1970s when the Tanzanian President Julius Nyerere strongly advocated it for the newly independent African countries. The fragility of these nations soon became obvious and was exposed in several lights: Dr. Hastings Kamuzu Banda of Malawi declared himself President-for-Life; In Lesotho, Prime Minister Leabua Jonathan voided the 1970 election which he had lost; King Sobhuza of Swaziland abolished the Parliament and the Constitution and reinstituted a monarchy. This was also the period when Zambia and Malawi were dissolving the Central African Federation coinciding with the merger of Tanganyika and Zanzibar to form present-day Tanzania. Large number of African States soon fell into Military dictatorship. In Nigeria, a series of events led to collapse of democratic institutions in 1966 and subsequently, a bitter Civil War.

Anytime I discuss the concept of nation building, I remember the poem by an Ugandan poet, Henry Barlow, Building the Nation,

> *Today I did my share*
> *In building the nation*
> *I drove a Permanent Secretary*
> *To an important and urgent function*
> *In fact to a luncheon at the Vic.*
>
> *The menu reflected its importance*
> *Cold Bell beer with small talk*
> *Then fried chicken with niceties*
> *Wine to fill the hollowness of the laughs*
> *Ice cream to cover the stereotype jokes*
> *Coffee to keep the PS awake on return Journey*
>
> *I drove the Permanent Secretary back*
> *He yawn many times in the back of the Car.*
> ....
>
> *So two nation builders*
> *Arrived home this evening*
> *With terrible stomach pains*
> *The result of building the nation-*
> *Different ways.*

From Barrow's poem, we can see how different people engage in nation building.

There is the usual temptation to reduce the meaning of Nation Building to: national integration, national development, political development, or the development of a national consciousness. The term includes all these, but to reduce it to any of them is to commit a "reductionist" fallacy. Simply put, it can mean the systematic process of making a people, who hitherto are from different cultural, ethnic, religious, racial, or national backgrounds to feel a sense of belonging together within a nation. Karl Deutch, in his book Nation Building identifies five stages of achieving this "systematic process".

First, the group exists as a tribe, with its distinct language and proud culture, and will resist any attempt to integrate it with other groups. The next stage is to incorporate them forcefully into other groups with the use of force. The third stage is for them to minimally accept, often with the use of force or the threat of it, the new arrangement by cooperating minimally. At the fourth stage, their level of resistance is reduced to the minimum and their cooperation and obedience have risen astronomically, though they still keep their cultural identities intact. The fifth is when the group becomes almost indistinguishable from other groups within the state. This is when total assimilation is achieved. The last two stages will require minimal use of force. As a post-colonial nation, the first three stages ended with colonialism. The last two have proven difficult in Nigeria, either due to deliberate colonial policy or shameless neglect by leaders at independence. A strong aspect of nation building is the fight against corruption. In all these, where and how does the church come in?

THE CHURCH AND THE WAR ON CORRUPTION

The Church has a great role to play in this serious fight against corruption. In this case, the Church must become partisan by standing against a corrupt government and for the ones that has a firm stance against corruption. The Church must re-create its role in the war against corruption beyond the level of theoretical teaching of moral principles. Under our theoretical teachings, it may appear obvious that it is clearly wrong to be corrupt. But experience has shown that corruption in Nigeria has taken so many forms that sometimes it is often no longer clear as we have argued in this book earlier. The Church's moral principles which are taught in Sunday school classes may be well known but what of their implementations? When a so-called Christian whose duty to award contracts in government offices engages in making money by inflating contracts, what should we call that? Is it that he or she does not know it is wrong to do such based on his moral conscience? Or are the messages he hears every Sunday in Church not enough? That is why the religious communities, especially the leaders, must constantly keep before the minds and hearts of their followers the truth about the moral life that people live.

The Church also must divest itself of materialism and look up towards what is above that simply the limited material gains of this world. We need to constantly remind our congregations that the fruit of corruption is only of temporary value and that the judgment of God catches up on everyone. We often say that "honesty is the best policy", and that indeed is true. We should continue to encourage our people to live honest lives, knowing that God blesses those who make effort and punishes sometimes even in this world those who live a life of iniquity.

According to Dr. Alan Geyer of the Washington National Cathedral in the United States, he argued that the Church as an institution is no stranger to the problems of corruption in its own sphere. They have held properties and investments that have exploited poor people, and often attempted to conceal such facts, and have coveted special political privileges contrary to the integrity of democratic institutions. However, in a deeper sense, the seriousness of Christianity about human sinfulness teaches much about corruption. While modern persons might cringe at the mention of notions such as original sin and human depravity, the history of this century demonstrates that human beings are capable of inhuman things. Democratic institutions must be structured with reference not only to the positive capacities of persons for self-government, but also to the propensity of persons to greed, hostility, cruelty and corruption. It is not enough to say that corruption threatens democracy. It must also be said that democracy will soberly expect corruption, but will design governmental structures and public strategies to cope with it. Some fundamentally positive perspectives deeply grounded in the Christian faith may help equip democratic leaders in efforts to combat corruption.

Also, the Bible recognizes that law alone is not enough to insure against corruption. Indeed, law, transparency, a free press, and even international conferences convened by senior political office holders are insufficient to prevent corrupt practice in the administration of justice. Even with all laws, there will still be those open to corruption, and those willing to corrupt. The law is too ungainly a tool to be successful alone in suppressing corruption in government. The ideal of fairness, and therefore intolerance for corruption, must be a manifest part of society at large. In all parts of the world, for Jewish, Christian, Hindu, Muslim or other religions, the ideals of fairness and honest service must be a part of the fabric of society. People of good will may disagree honestly about what God commands, but we must follow the sense of the commandment to justice because it serves us well as humans, and we must teach our children to follow it as well.

When we speak of the role of the Church or faith community in the fight against corruption, we are stressing in particular the role of religion and the spiritual dimension of life in the war against corruption. Religion in itself never goes around on its own; it is people who express religious ideas and not the other way round. Religion has to do first and foremost with the relationship of humanity with God. All great religions have a strong conviction not only that we do have access to God in our prayer but that we are made up of both body and soul, material and spiritual. In the Christian perspective, we believe that our life on earth should already begin to forge a close relationship with God, a relationship which will continue when we die. We call this "eternal life", which is understood as communion with God. Religion therefore, deals with the whole person both body and soul, whether in the here and now or in the hereafter. That is why religious communities do not restrict their activities to only organize prayers and other purely religious matters. We also get engaged in programs of human development, in the areas of education, health, human promotion and so on.

With regard to the topic of this chapter, it is important also to highlight the fact that for Christians, religion involves man both as individual and in his social dimension. It is therefore not a matter of "me and my God". The most basic prayer of the Christian faith is the 'Our Father'. We address God not as "my Father" but as the father of all. That is also why the Christian community is organized into religious communities, whether in terms of denominations or ecclesiastical jurisdictions within the same denomination.

Sometimes, it is alleged that religious communities are themselves mainly responsible for corruption in our society because they are said to accept dishonest funds from people who are corrupt. While this may look true in some cases, it is not true for others. It is possible that some religious leaders may indeed be aiding and abetting corruption in this way. But in such a case, they are only being humans. There are bad eggs among all human groups. But I do not know of any religion that condones in principle the practice of corruption in any form.

However, we cannot close our eyes to the fact that many of those who donate big sums to churches and mosques may not have accumulated their wealth in a transparent and just way. Where this is clearly the case, it is the duty of the religious leader not to welcome such donations. God cannot be bribed. For instance, if someone comes to me and says 'Pastor, I have come to thank God for the success of a fraudulent contract last week, here is N2 million being tithe from the N2 billion that was the value of the contract" I will tell such a person to return all the money stolen from government coffers. To accept the donation under those terms will obviously be "aiding and abetting" corruption. In fact, to deliberately and knowingly accept and keep stolen goods is to steal. That is why the foreign bankers who accept and keep the loot of our corrupt leaders are themselves thieves. However, when people bring donations to the church, I have a right to presume that they have come in good faith and with a clear conscience. We would have done our duty if we consistently teach and warn people that God cannot be bribed. Everyone will have to settle his/her case with God. We could add also in this connection that the church often carries out social programs and projects for the common good of citizens. Indeed one of the reasons why the church collects money is precisely to be able to do charity to the poor. It can be said that the dishonest person who steals from public funds could indeed try, through such donations, to make restitution back to the society for what has been dishonestly taken away.

Corruption is a common denominator in our society today. It is not restricted to any particular religion. Therefore, we all have a common battle. Interestingly, our religious principles and holy books practically coincide in this matter 'Thou Shalt not Steal' is valid both for all religious faiths. That being the case, this is an area where we can surely join hands together to send out clear and joint messages condemning corruption in all its forms. We should also be able to work together among the different religious bodies on concrete practical anti-corruption programs.

In some cases, as we have seen in recent times, we might be tempted to protect and cover up our members who fall foul of the law because "he is our man". Of course it is our duty to minister unto members of our flock even when they are under accusation of corruption. But that is a different matter from "white-washing" them and openly defending them, as if we want to constitute ourselves into an obstacle in the fight against corruption. It is not difficult for a prudent religious leader to know how far to go in this matter.

Unfortunately, for many decades, government and her agencies seem to have difficulties in relating well and working with religious organizations. This was not so in earlier times. We believe it is about time that government agencies seek deliberate channels for welcoming the open hands of collaboration which faith based organizations and religious groups are constantly offering. The fight against corruption is one such area for collaboration.

WHAT THE CHURCH SHOULD BE DOING

First, we must come to terms with the fact that the Church should preach repentance and forgiveness. Let us be clear. Corruption is a sin. It has no other name. Unlike other sins, corruption is a sin against the nation, the state or the institution against which it was committed in the first instance. There are sins against other human beings. There are sins against the spirit. There are also sins against the flesh. Corruption or corrupt acts are sins against the properly constituted authority of the state.

Viewed in this perspective, the Church must make people realize that whoever engages in corrupt deals does so against an entire people.

Since corruption kills, when as a result of corruption either due to over-invoicing or poor supervision or execution of, say, road contracts led to the death of many people, the offender in this case has blood in his hands. Not the blood of one, but of many that have died as a result of his selfish behavior.

When there is sin, there is also forgiveness. But we should understand forgiveness in the right perspective. When you offend me, as Sunday Adelaja, say you stole my money. I can choose to forgive you and tell you to go and sin no more. That is a personal offence. When you offend the church by stealing or embezzling Church funds, that is no longer a personal offence, it has become institutional. It will take the church to forgive the offender in that case, not Pastor Adelaja. Any offence against the spirit can only be forgiven by God Himself. In the same light, offences against the nation are to be forgiven by the entire people against whom it was committed in the first instance.

Let us give an example here. Mr. Ajasa stays in a neighborhood with two families and two bachelors. Unknown to him, he woke up one morning and could not get water to have his bath. He checked everywhere he could not find any so he decided to use a bucket of water belonging to Mr. Ajagbe with the understanding that the latter will not be going to work that day and he would have gotten his bucket of water back for him before he wakes up. Unfortunately for him, Mr. Ajagbe was up before he finished having his bath. Ajasa could only imagine the worse when he heard from the bathroom that Ajagbe was looking for his bucket of water. Why should he have used the water without informing the owner? On the promise that he will get another bucket for Ajagbe, tensions dowsed and everyone went to work that morning with Ajagbe deciding to forgive Ajasa.

Later in the afternoon, Ajasa, a commercial tricycle driver, committed a traffic offence of disobeying the traffic light and hitting a pregnant woman. He was taken to the nearest police station for interrogation. On getting to the station, he met Ajagbe, a police inspector, who is to preside at his case!

Since he has been living in the compound, at no time has he seen Inspector Ajagbe in uniform let alone knowing he was a police officer. The moment of truth came. Since they stayed in the same compound, he thought Ajagbe should come to his rescue.

At that point, Inspector Ajagbe told him that though he offended him that morning using his bucket of water, he has since forgiven him. On his violation of the traffic offence, it was not an offence against him but against the pregnant woman and the state!

The problem I think we are having most of the time is that we tend to think that corruption is a personal offence. When we make people realise that corruption is a public offence, they will learn to behave. Like Ajagbe in our story, the Church must let people confess the sins they committed against the public in PUBLIC before we can talk about forgiveness!

It is tempting to try to explain away our sins or blame others or blame the devil. We may rationalize that committing a sin is okay because some greater good or lesser evil will result. We may rationalize our greed and lack of compassion for others. We may use our own weaknesses as an excuse for not trying harder. We may convince ourselves that a sin does not matter as long as no one knows about it. We may argue that revenge is justified to punish an offender. We may rationalize our sinful actions by inventing false motives to justify them. We may rationalize that a half truth is not an actual lie.

Common excuses when people are caught in corrupt acts include, "Everyone else is doing it," "It's not technically illegal," "He did it to me," "No one will know," "The ends justify the means," "It's for a good cause," "It wasn't my fault," "I couldn't help it," "There are worse things," "They are just as bad," "He had it coming," "I deserve it," "It worked out for the best," "I don't have the abilities or money that other people have," "I have my rights," "It's for his own good," "They've got more than I do," "It's a bad law," "It's a stupid rule," "I am what I am," "It's never been a problem before," "What they don't know won't hurt them," "It's too hard," "Nobody cares," "Nobody will miss it," "It doesn't hurt anybody," "God made me this way," and many others.

Only recently, a Catholic priest attached to the Catholic Diocese of Jalingo in Taraba state, Rev Fr Charles Nyameh, advised treasury looters in Nigeria to return their loots in exchange for God's mercies. The priest supported his call with the story of Zacchaeus, a rich tax collector in the Bible, who encountered Jesus, repented of his evil deeds and his sins were forgiven.

We should recall that Zacchaeus' encounter with Jesus led to his repentance and promise to make restitution of what he stole from others.

In our own case our public and political servants, who know they acquired their wealth in a corrupt manner, I am joining my voice with the priest, should follow Zacchaeus example and make restitution of what they stole from our collective wealth.

God will not let go of all those who stole our resources and corruptly enrich themselves. He is calling on all of us to make restitution for our wrong actions to enjoy his mercies. This is, and should be, the message the Church and religious leaders should be preaching. The "get rich quick" messages most religious leaders are preaching today fuels desperation and tendencies for corruption. We should make the people realize they are committing sin against the nation and against God

The Church must also propagate the right values. This is not only limited to the Church but mosques and traditional institutions as well. We must sing this as songs in agencies of government, public places and anytime we have the opportunity to speak at government functions. We must register our support for the anti-corruption drive and initiatives.

The story is told of Doug Abner of the Appalachian Center for Transformation. Mr. Doug was a local pastor who helped lead the charge throughout Manchester's transformation. He tells of how unbelief and fear had crippled the church prior to the march in 2004. Due to the years of corruption of local officials and the rigged election system, believers felt helpless in making any changes. The lack of unity among churches only strengthened the resolve of corrupt officials to intimidate and threaten anyone who challenged their agenda. Even so, Abner shares that the day after the march, these same believers, now emboldened in their faith, came together to do something radical.

Instead of launching campaigns against the officials or publicly decrying their unlawful deeds, these believers went to the offices of these city officials with gifts of potted plants and asked if they could pray for them. One of these corrupt officials had previously threatened a pastor and his church. To their amazement, this official called in his staff and allowed Abner to lead them in prayer. Years later, this same official would confess Jesus as Lord and ask for forgiveness. The fear of the Lord was so prevalent; those involved in illegal activities began to turn on each other. As believers continued to pray and work together, God battled on their behalf. Even as the opposition continued, churches in the community began to see a dramatic increase of salvations and the favor of God came upon the local church. Their unified stand and resolve to do things Gods way was paying off. If the Church adopts this method in Nigeria, we will do more in helping to win the anti-corruption war.

The Church is at a similar place of opportunity. We have seen God work on our behalf in the past and now we must get involved in the decision making process. Rather than simply criticizing the opposition through social media, we need to act. God's favor is already at work and we must seize the opportunity to demonstrate the power of the kingdom through our witness and our work. It starts at the community level where everyone can participate and make a difference.

The challenges before us are bigger than the Aso Rock. The ingrained belief systems and mindsets of rebellion and godlessness must be shifted and displaced by a people of God's power and presence. It is only as we step up and actively engage in our fields of influence that we can make any lasting difference for the kingdom.

For the anti-corruption drive of the Federal Government to be effective, it must begin from the grassroots and Nigerians must stop pointing accusing fingers at politicians and leaders, because they evolved from families and communities. In this, the church and religious bodies play a critical role in mobilizing the masses at the grassroots through sensitization and public communication.

We are only scratching the surface when we fight corruption from the top, because corruption is with us everywhere we turn: the gate man in the government ministry, driver, cashier, petroleum attendant and the mechanic that repairs cars.

CHAPTER ELEVEN

Nigeria: A Sleeping Lion

In this chapter, we shall be looking at the hidden and manifest potentials of Nigeria. What is holding us back to be in our rightful place in the comity of developed nations? Why can Nigeria not overtake the US economy?

THE METAPHOR OF THE LION

The 1994 award-winning American animated epic movie, The Lion King, produced by Walt Disney Pictures tells the amazing story of Simba. Simba is a young lion who is to succeed his father, Mufasa, as King of the Pride Lands; however, after Simba's uncle Scar murders Mufasa, Simba is manipulated into thinking he was responsible and flees into exile. Upon maturation living with two wastrels, Simba is given some valuable perspective from his childhood friend, Nala, and his shaman, Rafiki, before returning to challenge Scar to end his tyranny and take his place in the Circle of Life as the rightful King.

During the story, we saw Simba collapsed in a desert and is rescued by Timon and Pumbaa, a meerkat and warthog who are fellow outcasts. Simba grows up in the jungle with his two new friends, living a carefree life under the motto "hakuna matata" (meaning "no worries" in Swahili). Now a young adult, Simba rescues Timon and Pumbaa from a hungry lioness who turns out to be Nala. She and Simba reunite and fall in love, and she urges him to return home, telling him the Pride Lands have become a drought-stricken wasteland under Scar's reign. Feeling guilty over his father's death, Simba refuses and storms off. He later encounters Rafiki, who tells him that Mufasa' spirit lives on in Simba. Simba is visited by the ghost of Mufasa in the night sky, who tells him he must take his rightful place as king. Realizing he can no longer run from his past, Simba decides to return home.

All the while, Simba living a life of "no worries" forgot who he was. He started behaving like his new friends, Timon and Pumbaa, who themselves lack ambitions. Not until when he met Nala did he come to the realization that he was indeed a lion and not just that, a lion king, where he truly belonged!

There is another story of a lion who mistook itself to be a sheep. It grew up in a flock of sheep and so he had no consciousness that he was a lion. He didn't know he was a lion. He would bleat like a sheep, he'd eat grass like a sheep. He will run from wolves and wild dogs. One day they were wandering at the edge of a big jungle when a mighty lion let out a big roar and leaped out of the forest and right into the middle of the flock. All the sheep scattered and ran away. Imagine the surprise of the jungle lion when he saw this other lion there among the sheep. So, he gave chase. He got hold of him. And there was this lion, cringing in front of the king of the jungle. And the jungle lion said to him, "What are you doing here?"

And the other lion said, "Have mercy on me. Don't eat me. Have mercy on me." But the king of the forest dragged him away saying "Come on with me." And he took him to a lake and he said, "Look." So, the lion who thought he was a sheep looked and for the first time he saw his reflection. He saw his image. Then he looked at the jungle lion, and he looked in the water again, and he let out a mighty roar. He was never a sheep again.

There are critical lessons we can learn from these two stories about Nigeria. We are a nation with full potentials to lead the black race. We have all the potentials to be among the most developed nations on earth, if not the best. We have all it takes to be king, like Simba, but we chose to live like outcasts even though no one is preventing us from achieving our potentials. How tragic it is to live our lives as a nation with less than our fullest potential explored and invested!

WHY NIGERIA'S ECONOMY CAN OVERTAKE AMERICA'S ECONOMY

According to a United Nations report in 2013 titled: **"World Population Prospects: The 2012 Revision"**, the world body claims that by the year 2050 which is about three decades away – the world will have two billion more people on it than it does today, and China will no longer be its largest country. In the said report, the most notable aspect of population growth is the developing world, which, to put it mildly, is expanding at a mind-boggling rate. While growth in the developed world is expected to remain flat, the population of developing regions is projected to soar from the current 5.9 billion to 8.2 billion in 2050.

Taking a quick look at some other projections from the report, the following came to surface:

- India's population will surpass that of China's around the year 2028, at 1.45 billion. Shortly after that, China's population will begin to decrease, shrinking to about 1.1 billion by the year 2100. India's will continue to rise for several more decades, however, before beginning its own gradual decline and hitting approximately 1.5 billion in 2100.

- By the middle of the 21st century, Nigeria will be a larger country than the United States, and by 2100 could be giving China a run for its money as the second-largest country in the world.

- More than half of the world's population growth between now and 2050 will occur in Africa. Outside of Africa, the rest of the world will grow by only about 10 percent between now and 2100.

- Europe will shrink by 14 percent between now and 2100. Almost none of Europe's countries are producing babies at a high enough rate to replace lost population.

- Globally, life expectancy is expected to soar in the coming decades. By 2045-2050, the average human being will live 76 years – approximately the life expectancy of the average U.S. citizen today. By the end of the century that figure will rise to 82 years (and in developed countries, to 89). Even in the world's least developed countries, the average citizen at the end of the century will live to see 78.

Given these figures, we can see that the Nigerian economy has all it takes to overtake the US economy by 2050. The truth of the matter is that we may not have to wait that long if we can take away the internal constraints preventing us to get there.

Throughout this book, we have identified just one challenge - corruption- as the main problem facing the Nigerian economy.

Our perspective to corruption is like that of a leaking container, mentioned in the beginning of this book. No matter how much water we pour into a leaking or punctured container, it will eventually turn empty, achieving nothing meaningful.

Even though some may argue for us to build a large economy through diversification, the result will remain the same- stagnation.

We are aware of those who will ask: *"Will fighting corruption feed the masses?"* or *"When there was no fight against corruption, were people not feeding well?"* the points, on the surface, look valid, but further analysis show how defective in logic such thoughts are.

First, fighting corruption does not feed the masses, at least not immediately. But, for the masses to eat tomorrow, we must fight corruption today. The funds that have been stolen through corruption do not trickle down to the masses, only the looters, and their families benefit from the loot. Let us look at the case of Andrew Yakubu, who hid the sum of $9.8 million USD in his house. Apart from his family, who benefits from the money?

Secondly, whatever "feeding" the masses get from looted funds, is only a Trojan horse. Gifts like Trojan Horses is not the type anyone will like to have because you get to pay more later. It is just like the wood-eating insect. It feeds on the wood to the extent the wood becomes useless. Unknown to it, the wood will die off and there will be nothing more to eat.

The recent case of James Ibori still amazes me. I met some who justify Ibori's actions because, according to him, *"He stole Delta state money."* I laughed. This man as governor of the state did not bother to construct the road in his village in Oghara. He shares money for people to eat today, forgetting about tomorrow. Alas, this is the logic of corruption.

With "today" mentality among many of our people, the chances of Nigeria overtaking the US economy appear slim.

POLITICAL LEADERSHIP AND CORRUPTION

That corruption is the bane of Nigeria's socio-economic development is to state the obvious.

Today, in Nigeria, there is a consensus among well-meaning individuals and foreign nations that corruption has inevitably become a major clog in the quest for sustainable growth and development. It is further agreed that it must be halted before it shuts down the country. It is the single most critical impediment to achieving the Sustainable Development Goals (SDGs); and like a deadly virus, it attacks the vital structures and systems that engender progressive functioning of the society. Like most developing countries, Nigeria is still grappling with the dilemma of corruption that has largely retarded social development, undermined economic growth, discouraged foreign investments and reduced the resources available for infrastructural development, public service, and poverty reduction programs. Much more disturbing, according to Nuhu Ribadu speaking at the 2007 edition of the Gani Fawehinmi Lecture, the scourge of corruption leaves the poor perpetually disproportionately under-privileged, even as it renders the development of democracy and the building of a society of opportunity more problematic. Thus, by diverting assets away from their intended use, corruption can be said to be the single most important factor responsible for the failure of governance and lack of sustainable socio-economic development in Nigeria.

Without doubt, the unpardonable failure of the political leadership class managing the affairs and wealth of the country had inevitably brought severe misery to many voiceless and helpless Nigerians. It must also be mentioned here that Nigeria's post-independence political bureaucratic and military elites had terribly pillaged the nation's common wealth and national patrimony with impunity, thereby denying Nigerians access to economic prosperity and quality living condition. Also disheartening, is the fact that the volume of development assistance totaling about $400 billion that flowed into the country for socio-economic development between independence and the collapse of military dictatorship in 1999 was atrociously squandered by the political leaders of the period. The mismanagement of resources of such quantum which was worth six times the resources committed to the rebuilding of Western Europe after a devastating Second World War simply defines the callousness of the political leadership towards the socio-economic wellbeing of the country.

A noticeable consequence of corruption on the political and economic wellbeing of Nigerians has been the distortion of governmental expenditure. This often results in diversion of public investment on large-scale projects, typically military or infrastructure projects, rather than on the provision of necessary public services such as health, roads, housing, and education. Mostly, the Nigerian government at all levels spends relatively more on large and hard-to-manage projects, such as airports or national stadia, to make room for fraud because execution of such project makes fraud easy. Consequently, according to Victor Dike, development projects are made unnecessarily complex so as to justify the corrupt huge expenses on them. This situation makes it inevitable for the limited but valuable fund earmarked for development to disappear into private pockets.

Indeed, it is difficult to think of any social ill in the country that is not traceable to the embezzlement and misappropriation of public funds, particularly as a direct or indirect consequence of the corruption perpetrated by the callous political leadership class since independence. The cycle of poverty keeps growing with all its attendant consequences even as the rate of unemployment remains perpetually high. By giving mediocrity advantage over intelligence through nepotism and cronyism, intellectual capital, which is the bulwark of development and advancement, has continued to drift abroad in search of greener pasture. Paradoxically, the scourge of corruption has left the country straddling two economic worlds at the same time. To state the obvious, the country has found itself in the quagmire of a country too rich to be poor and at the same time too poor to be rich. Thus, this has made it inevitable for every Nigerian to be a victim of corruption.

As a consequence of unparalleled and unrivalled corruption in Nigeria, the healthcare delivery system and the education sector have become comatose and are nearing total collapse. Government spending has been considerably reduced towards these vital social sectors of the economy and others of equal importance, which are supposed to be of high priority to government. To this end, the resultant effects have been catastrophic as different forms of malpractices and corrupt practices have rubbished the Nigerian educational system, which is perceived from the outside as inadequate and, its product, substandard. More so, corruption in the health sector has also given room for counterfeit and adulterated drugs to find easy passage into the country with little or no resistance until 1999 when Professor Dora Akunyili took over the leadership of the National Agency for Food and Drug Administration and Control (NAFDAC). It would be recalled that her first point of duty was an attempt to eradicate fake and adulterated drugs. This effort almost cost her life when gunmen suspected to have been sent by importers of fake and adulterated drugs attacked her in 2005. Infrastructural facilities have long been in an abysmal state and to shore up its dwindling income, much of which was embezzled under successive governments and siphoned to foreign bank accounts, government resorted to excessive taxation of the already economically deprived and impoverished populace.

Perhaps the most tragic effect of corruption on Nigeria has been the failure of the country to attain its economic potentials. Despite its substantial natural and human resources, Nigeria remains desperately poor due to bad management of its wealth by successive corrupt governments. Today, Nigeria is one of the poorest countries in the world per capita. Its unadjusted GNP per capita of $300 leaves it in 164th position among other countries in 1999. The per capita GNP PPP (purchasing power parity) figure of $820 looks better at first glance but it ranks 199th out of the 209 countries covered according to the World Bank's 2000 World Development Report in 2001 titled, Attacking Poverty. In 2010, Nigeria's GDP per capita (PPP) of $2,365 ranked as 138th in the world out of the 180 countries, while the GNI per capita (PPP) of $2,160 left the country in the 172nd position out of the 215 countries listed in the World Development Indicators Database in 2011. These are not just abstract statistics. An average Nigerian leads an appallingly difficult life that is worse in most ways than the situations in other Third World countries. Unfortunately, the country has not been able to breakthrough with any significant step that would dramatically improve the living conditions of its mostly impoverished population due to the high level of corruption in the system.

SOME THOUGHTS ON LEADERSHIP

My purpose in this section is to share some personal thoughts on leadership taking in retrospect the role of the youths and other Nigerians especially in the fight against corruption and their contributions to nation-building. I have been strongly influenced by two great books: Chief Obafemi Awolowo's Thoughts on Nigerian Constitution and Dr. Deepak Chopra's The Soul of Leadership. For most Nigerians the latter author is unfamiliar.

While I may not, unlike many other people fully cast aspersion totally on political leadership as we also will have to take some strokes for the country's woes. Chief Awolowo strongly criticizes Nigerian Leaders in his book for lacking "...*comprehension, mental magnitude, and spiritual depth.*" He went further to say:

BY COMPREHENSION, WE MEAN THE ABILITY OF A MAN TO APPRECIATE AND GRASP THE SALIENT DETAILS, AS WELL AS MOST OF THE PRACTICAL AND TEMPORAL IMPLICATIONS OF A GIVEN PROBLEM OR SITUATION.

AWOLOWO, 1966:158

In simple terms, Nigerian leaders lack common sense on how to run the country. In reading Awo's statements, recent events in the country come to mind: Missing $20 billion from NNPC coffers under the full glare of the Ministry of Petroleum Resources; Incessant attacks of malignant Boko Haram mainly in the North-East with the Government looking hapless; the fatal Nigerian Immigration Service recruitment exercise; Multi-billion naira private Jets of some Ministers (no big deal...); Multi-billion naira Police pension Fund scam (and all is well) etc. I doubt if any day passes without any report of these in the media.

As the old English saying goes," *Show me your friend and I will tell you who you are"* should be reframed *"Show me your leader and I will tell you who you are."* This therefore shows that leaders and followers co-create each other. There can be no leadership without follow-ership and the reverse is also true. In his wonderful book, The Wretched of the Earth, the French-born Algerian statesman, Frantz Fanon argued that ultimately the people get the kind of leaders they deserve; and the leaders deserve the kind of followers they get. After all, a leader is anyone called to guide, teach, command, motivate, inspire or plan. By this, we all are leaders.

The National Association of Nigerian Students (NANS) had a glorious past in the 1960s and 70s even the 80s due to its strong stance in defense of interests of Students and the downtrodden in the society. But what went wrong suddenly? Today it is difficult to distinguish between a Political Party's Convention and that of NANS. So where are the leaders of tomorrow?

Like NANS, a University Campus branch of the Non-Academic Staff Union of Universities and Other Educational Institutions (NASU) did something quite amusing. The members' monetized benefits were allegedly cornered by the Vice Chancellor thus provoking the Union to embark on an indefinite strike. It is instructive to know that the Union leader, on being promoted by the University Management from level 4 to 7 arbitrarily abandoned the poor members and mortgaged their futures for personal ambition. Do we still have the moral authority to question our leaders when they collect huge World Bank/IMF loans and these never get home?

Leadership is about dynamism. If we continue to use the same old responses, worn-out theories, old failed approaches instead of creating new ones we honestly aren't expecting things to change. I am sure no one recalls experiencing bomb blasts being a daily practice two decades ago. These are the realities we live by in Nigeria today. But to respond with an overtly short-staffed, ill-equipped security agencies to a fire-emitting Boko Haram is to say the least crooked thinking. The Americans were told in clear language that they were in the 21st Century and no longer the Civil War, Cold war, Vietnam, or Gulf War Years of the 20th Century during the 9/11 attacks. Robert Green in his book, The 33 Strategies of War noted that there is nothing good that comes out of fighting the last war.

Thirdly, true leadership deals with Visions. Without visions they say our people perish. Great leaders are defined by their visions. I am impressed by Chief Awolowo's vision for introducing Free Education Policy in the Old Western Region in 1955 and the establishment of the University of Ife, now Obafemi Awolowo University, Ile-Ife (those that have visited the Campus can attest to its uniqueness). I am equally marveled by Mallam Aminu Kano's vision for the 'Talakawas' in the North. Apart from these two and a little others, Nigeria has been unfortunate to have visionless and unprepared people as leaders since independence. Since these leaders aren't prepared in the first instance, they turn out poor policies, programs even the critical decision they take becomes suspect.

Nigerians woke up on Monday 14th April, 2014 to receive the news of bomb blast in Abuja the nation's

Capital. The second day there was the news of the kidnaping of about 200 female students at Government Girls Secondary School in Chibok, Borno State. The question then is with all the Security gadgets we claim to parade we still cannot contain this menace? I ask because it appears to me that we are confused. Nobody wants to look stupid in public glare.

The truth of the matter is that a confused leader cannot lead effectively, just as a divided, unfocused, disorganized and disoriented people cannot follow. The latter is being taken advantage of by unscrupulous politicians for cheap political gains. So, leaders and followers are not independent of each other.

Only clear-headed persons can effectively lead. But ordinary clear-headedness without visions is like tea without sugar. Since the needs of today are not necessarily those of tomorrow, good leaders try to phantom them in advance to avoid creating a vacuum. It is this lack of vision that made countries like Ghana to do better than we are presently doing. Great visionaries like Awolowo and the like presently elude us.

Great leaders must know what role to play per time. They must be able to discern the role they play in every situation. At war time he is the Commander-in-Chief or Chief Security Officer; at peace time he is the Father of the Nation, shunning partisanship in any form; during the period of division he is the Uniting figure and so on. In Nigeria, it appears our leaders don't know what role is expected of them per time. It is for this reason they get poor advice from their Advisors who are only bent on flattering their Master's egos.

Great leaders spend their time understanding the needs of their people. When others are bothered about winning the next election, or their party, or tribal origin, they do their best to satisfy their people. They are like marketers who are to satisfy the needs of their customers, to guarantee their loyalty. It was this great truth that Franklin D. Roosevelt understood, as US President during the Great Depression (1929-1933), when he chose to pitch his tent with the poor who were most affected during this period. For these acts, he was rewarded with great victories in four consecutive elections which are unprecedented and unsurpassed in US history. This was what led the great political leader and perhaps the most influential religious figure in World Civilizations, Amenhotep IV, Pharaoh of Egypt (1360-1350BC) to say: *"The glory of a King is the welfare of his people; his power and dominion resteth on the hearts of his subjects."* The greatest leaders have taken heed of this eternal truth.

Also, the greatest leaders are not those that lead from the mountains. They pay attention to the deepest levels of human experience. They don't make themselves super humans. In essence they are humble. It becomes very difficult to see situations clearly when one is surrounded by such luxury Nigerian leaders are infected with. All these rather make people blind hence they depend on second hand reports from their unreliable lieutenants.

When Awo opined, in his Thoughts on Nigerian Constitution, that great leaders have "vanquished the emotions of greed and fear..." he only meant that Great leaders are fearless and less emotional. He opined: *"...we are sexually continent, abstemious in food, abstain totally from alcoholic beverage and tobacco..."* To show how reckless and impulsive our political leaders are. Millions of naira goes into their personal consumption and house keeps daily in a country where millions of people go to bed on empty stomachs. One then wonders whether they consume this much in their private lives! They are okay advising the people to make sacrifices that they themselves would never make.

Great leaders on the other hand give everything, and I mean everything in the service of their people. They are ready even at the cost of their lives, to take decisions that benefit their people. To them leadership is sacrifice. They lead by examples. They will never tell their people to do what they themselves cannot do. They will not live in affluence when their people live in abject poverty. Invariably, they live a much disciplined life.

Mao Tse-tung during the Great March (1934) led the Chinese Communists in a tedious, dangerous and life-threatening journey through the vast country. In this journey, Chairman Mao went through what every last Communist went through in the jungle as they walked. He ensured that everyone has eaten before taking his turn. With this level of discipline they were able to defeat the more organized, well-financed, and well-trained Nationalists. The Communists successfully captured power in 1949 and have been there ever since.

History is not in want of leaders whom gave their lives in the service of their people: Mahatma Gandhi(India), Abraham Lincoln(USA), John F. Kennedy(USA), Patrice Lumumba(Congo), Malcom Little "X" (USA), Martin Luther King(USA), Ernesto "Che" Guevara(Argentina), Amilcar Cabral(Guinea-Bissau), Salvador Allende(Chile), Murtala Muhammed (Nigeria) and many others. Others have endured painful punishments and assaults: Nelson Mandela (South Africa), Denis Brutus (South African Poet), Fidel Castro (Cuba), Juan and Evita Peron(Argentina) and others all paid the ultimate price for their people. Others like Ahmed Ben Bella (Algeria) and Kwame Nkrumah(Ghana) were exiled from their countries due to their defense of their people.

We are indeed in a period of great triumphs and potential pitfalls. The World is in dear need for both leadership and followership. To make the difference, the leaders must set the pace for the followers. The World is in desperate need of Inspirational leaders, not necessarily politicians. That is why as our young people we must set the pace. In the war to get our nation back, we must make crucial sacrifices. We all have to. There is no "savior" anywhere that will come and help us if we are not ready to help ourselves. There are no "X-Men" specially trained that will come to our aid. We have to do it ourselves, and it starts now. First, we must win the war against corruption no matter the costs!

From our survey of the Nigerian economy, we can see that the key problem is corruption generated especially by the political leadership. Corruption has attained an unimaginable height and is currently assuming a pandemic proportion in Nigeria through, and with the full support of the political leadership class since independence. Obviously, as a nation, we cannot move on without looking back because a people without a history can be compared to a tree without roots. The fact is obvious that there really was never a golden age of great leadership in the history of Nigeria. The lack of competent, responsible leaders with integrity, vision, high moral values has been the bane of the country. It is simply disheartening that Nigeria, a country blessed with natural resources and manpower is now doomed with uncertainty where abject poverty, high unemployment rate, looting and squandering of public funds, and the likes, all as a consequence of corruption, have become the order of the day.

No doubt, corrupt practices among the political leadership class have also resulted in undermining the growth and stability of the nation's trading and financial system. As Nigeria seeks for more Foreign Direct Investments (FDIs), corruption tends to thrive more and impede the country's ability to attract overseas capital. Corruption has also damaged economic development and reforms and if adequate care is not taken, it can hinder the nation's capacity to achieve any meaningful progress in the future.

Although the situation looked very despondent, it is not beyond remedy. To achieve this, there must be a complete change of attitude on the part of the Nigerian political leadership and the followership, because no matter how perfect or excellent the Constitution or other instruments for ensuring accountability and checking corruption in the country might be, all will come to naught unless the political leadership show the political will to abide by and enforce them. Consequently, until political and higher bureaucratic appointments ceases to be a means to easy accumulation of illicit wealth and a new political culture that abhors corruption in public life and humiliates corrupt public servant, emerge in Nigeria, the country cannot escape the inevitable disastrous consequences that comes with pervasive corruption.

In the final analysis, Nigeria simply has been lacking in one thing that every nation, big or small, needs to achieve greatness – credible, responsible and people-oriented leadership. After decades of failed attempts to produce credible leaders, it is imperative now for the political leadership to turn a new leave by rejecting old habits of corruption which has hitherto hindered Nigeria from becoming a modern, great, and developed nation. This is not in any way to undermine the need for strong institutions. Nevertheless, no country can develop strong institutions without the benefits of good leadership, leaders who will create the conditions necessary for building and sustaining strong institutions. A positive change in the attitudes of the Nigerian leadership class is all that is needed to end corruption in Nigeria and for the nation and its people to experience sustainable socio-economic development.

CONCLUSION

This book on how the Nigerian economy can overtake America's economy is simply a book to open the eyes of my countrymen to how much evil corruption has brought upon the most populous black nation in the world. It is my hope that I have been able to raise the awareness of Nigerians in this book to why each and every Nigerian must join the fight against corruption.

So why such a title for this book? Is it just to sell copies of the book? No sir! As I have explained in the book, if the total amount of money that has been stolen from the country is $20 trillion, that amount by itself is already bigger than the size of the US economy which is $17 trillion. So if that amount had remained in Nigeria's economy, Nigeria could have well become the China of Africa, competing well with the biggest economies in the world.

If we are going to count how much was lost, only during the government of President Jonathan, then it becomes easy to believe the calculations done by the former Governor of the Central bank of Nigeria Prof. Chukwuma Soludo. He alleged that 30 trillion Naira (the equivalent of 200 billion USD in 2013) was lost to corruption in Nigeria. This is only in 6 years of President Jonathan's government, from the year 2009 – 2015.

To put that in perspective, the amount of money Nigeria lost in 6 years is bigger than the whole economy of the Ukraine $177 billion, Kuwait $175 billion, Libya $74 billion, Hungary $133 billion, Morocco $114 billion, Romania $189 billion, Belarus $71 billion, Syria $71 billion, Angola $124 billion and Vietnam $171 billion etc. according to the 2013 world Bank statistics for nominal GDP of countries.

Remember we are only talking about the amount Nigeria lost in the oil sector. Let me even make it clearer. According to the 2013 World Bank reports, that amount of $200 billion we lost in 6 years is 4 times the whole economy of Ghana $48 billion, 4 times that of Ethiopia $47 billion, 4 times that of Tunisia $46 billion and Kenya $55 billion.

It gets more interesting, let me bring it closer to home and compare this amount to the GDP of some countries where Nigerians now run to as economic refugees. The lost $200 billion USD equivalent as at 2013 we are talking about is 6 times the budget of Cameroon $30 billion, 10 times the size of the economy of Zambia $20 billion, 10 times the economy of Uganda $19 billion, 10 times the economy of Gabon $19 billion, 14 times the economy of Senegal $14 billion, Botswana $14 billion, Jamaica $14 billion, republic of Congo $13 billion, equatorial Guinean $14 billion and Mozambique $14 billion according to World Bank GDP report by countries 2013.

The amount we lost in 6 years is half of the whole economy (GDP) of South Africa, Denmark, Venezuela, Colombia, Thailand, Austria, Iran, United Arab Emirates, and Malaysia. Oh my God!!! What a country we would have built if not for the monster of corruption!

MUCH FOOD IS IN THE FALLOW GROUND OF THE POOR, AND FOR LACK OF JUSTICE THERE IS WASTE.

PROV. 13:23

I again want to sue this opportunity to call on all conscientious Nigerians everywhere to individually take upon themselves the responsibility of ridding Nigeria of corruption. If not for ourselves, let us do it for the sake of our children and posterity.

Now I hope you understand why this book caries this title. It is not only our potential, it is also our future. Yes, we have not been able to build an economy to rival America's economy but we still have that potential if we will fight the menace of corruption that we have within us. We stand a good chance of building Nigeria into the next wonder of the world. May God help us.

For the Love of God, Church and Nation

References, Works Cited And Credits

Drew, E. (1999) The Corruption of American Politics. New York: The Overlook Press.

Dike, V. (2003) Corruption in Nigeria: A New Paradigm for Effective Control. Africa Economic Analysis. Available at www. AfricaEconomicAnalysis.org.

Vangard, The (2016, December 23) 'Politicians flock to London for Ibori', p. 40.

Afeikhena, Jerome. 2005. Managing Oil Rent for Sustainable Development and Poverty Reduction in Africa. Paper presented at the UNU-WIDER Jubilee Conference: Thinking Ahead: The Future of Development Economics, Helsinki. http://www.wider. unu.edu/conferece/conference-2005-3/conference.

Achebe, C (1983) An Image of Africa. London: Penguin.

Commission for Africa. 2005. Our Common Interest: Report of the Commission for Africa. London: HMG.

Osaghae, Eghosa. 1998. Nigeria since Independence: Crippled Giant. London: Hurst and Company.

Roberts, S. (2015, October 14) 'Diepreye Alamieyeseigha, Nigerian Notorious for Corruption, Dies at 62' New York Times. Accessed on http://www.nytimes.com/2015/10/15/world/diepreye-alamieyeseigha-nigerian-ex-governor-dies-at-62.html?_r=0 Retrieved on 29 December, 2016.

Rasheed, Sadig. 1995. Corruption, Ethics, and Accountability in Africa: Toward a Responsive Agenda for Action. In Corruption, Democracy and Human Rights in Southern Africa, edited by Ayodele Aderinwale, 43–63. Abeokuta: African Leadership Forum.

Transparency International, (2006) Global Corruption Barometer. www.transparency.org

Bailey, F.G. (1980) Stratagems and Spoils, Oxford: Basil Blackwell

Obasanjo, O. (1999) Inaugural Address, May 29

Klitgaard, R.(1988). Controlling Corruption. Berkeley: University of California Press.

Mauro, Paolo. 2002. Corruption and the Composition of Government Expenditure. In Governance, Corruption and

Economic Performance, edited by G. T. Abed and S. Gupta, 197–224. Washington, D.C.:International Monetary Fund.

Tanzi, Vito. 1998. Corruption around the World: Causes, Consequences, Scope and Cures. IMF staff papers, 45(4):559–594.

Omotola, Shola. 2006. The Next Gulf? Oil Politics, Environmental Apocalypse and Rising Tension in the Niger Delta region. ACCORD Occasional Paper Series, 1(3):3–31.

Amnesty International. 2005. Amnesty International Report 2005—Nigeria. 25 May. Available at: http://www.unhcr.org/refworld/docid/429b27f014.html.

Ibeanu, Okechukwu. 2000. Oiling the Friction: Environmental Conflict Management in the Niger Delta, Nigeria. Environmental Change and Security Project Report 6. Washington, D.C.: WoodrowWilson Center.

UNDP (United Nations Development Program). 2006. Niger Delta Human Development Report. Abuja: UNDP.

Ihonvbere, Julius and Shaw, Timothy. 1998. Illusions of Power: Nigeria in Transition. Trenton, N.J.: Zed Books.

National Committee on Corruption and Other Economic Crimes, 1990. Report, Lagos: Federal Government Printers

Central Bank of Nigeria(1983), AnnualReport and Statement of Accounts for the YearEnding 31 December, 1983, Lagos, Central Bank of Nigeria.

World Bank, (1997), Helping Countries Combat Corruption,Washington, DC, World Bank.

Ribadu, N. (2007, January). Corruption and Survival of Nigeria. Being a paper delivered at the Second Chief Gani Fawehinmi Annual Lectures/Symposium, Lagos.

World Bank. (2001). World Development Report (WDR 2000/2001): Attacking Poverty. Geneva:World Bank.

World Bank. (2011). World Development Indicators Database (July and August).

DFID (2015) Why corruption matters: understanding causes, effects and how to address them, Evidence Paper on Corruption [online]. Available from: https://www.gov.uk/government/uploads/system/uploads/attachment_data/file/406346/corruption-evidence-paper-why-corruption-matters.pdf [Accessed 3 March 2017].

World Bank Group, Making politics work for development: Harnessing transparency and citizen engagement, p.183. Available from: http://documents.worldbank.org/curated/en/268021467831470443/pdf/106337-revised-PUBLCI-Making-Politics-Work-for-Development.pdf [Accessed 3 March 2017].

Deane, James "The role of independent media in curbing corruption in fragile settings" BBC Media Action, Policy Briefing #16.

Rose-Ackerman, S. (1999), Corruption and Government: Causes, Consequences and Reform, Cambridge University Press, Cambridge.

Ezekwesili, O. 28 August 2012. Corruption, National Development, the Bar and the Judiciary. Abuja: 52nd Annual General Meeting (AGM) of the Nigerian Bar Association.

United Nations Economic Commission for Africa (UNECA). February 2015. Track it. Stop it. Get it: Report of the High Level Pane on Illicit Finance Flows from Africa. Africa: UNECA. Available [online] (http://www.uneca.org/sites/default/files/PublicationFiles/ iff_main_report_26feb_en.pdf).

World Bank. (2016, 12 January). GDP per Capita: Nigeria and Singapore (1960–2014). Available [online] (https://goo.gl/LNl6ez).

Bolashodun, Oluwatobi (2016, September 9), "President Buhari launches national re-orientation campaign", Naij. Accessed on https://politics.naij.com/960954-breaking-presient-buhari-launches-changebeginswithme-campaign-abuja.html

United Nations (2013). "World Population Prospects: The 2012 Revision." United Nations Headquarters, New York. Accessed on https://africacheck.org/wp-content/uploads/2014/10/World-Population-Prospect-2012-revision_upload-to-AC.pdf

PwC (2016). Impact of Corruption on Nigeria's Economy. Lagos: PricewaterhouseCoopers Limited

Awolowo, O. (1966) Thoughts on Nigerian Constitution. Oxford: Oxford University Press

Anisiudo, Mary-Ann Nkolikamma (2016) Cost of Students' Senior Secondary Education in Anambra State, Nigeria Unpublished MSc Thesis, Nnamdi Azikiwe University, Awka.

END NOTES

1. Mauro, Paolo. 2002. Corruption and the Composition of Government Expenditure. In Governance, Corruptionand Economic Performance, edited by G. T. Abed and S. Gupta, 197–224. Washington, D.C.:International Monetary Fund.

2. Tanzi, Vito. 1998. Corruption around the World: Causes, Consequences, Scope and Cures. IMF staff papers,45(4):559–594.

3. Omotola, Shola. 2006. The Next Gulf? Oil Politics, Environmental Apocalypse and Rising Tension in theNiger Delta. ACCORD Occasional Paper Series, 1(3):3–31.

4. Ibeanu, Okechukwu. 2000. Oiling the Friction: Environmental Conflict Management in the Niger Delta,Nigeria. Environmental Change and Security Project Report 6. Washington, D.C.: WoodrowWilson Center.

5. Ihonvbere, Julius and Timothy Shaw. 1998. Illusions of Power: Nigeria in Transition. Trenton, N.J.: ZedBooks.

6. Data supplied in Rose-Ackerman, S. (1999), Corruption and Government: Causes, Consequences and Reform,- Cambridge University Press, Cambridge.

7. DFID (2015) Why corruption matters: understanding causes, effects and how to address them, Evidence Paper on Corruption [online]. Available from: https://www.gov.uk/government/uploads/system/uploads/attachment_data/file/406346/corruption-evidence-paper-why-corruption-matters.pdf [Accessed 2 August 2016].

8. World Bank Group, Making politics work for development: Harnessing transparency and citizen engagement, p.183. Available from: http://documents.worldbank.org/curated/en/268021467831470443/pdf/106337-revised-PUBLCI-Making-Politics-Work-for-Development.pdf [Accessed 1 August 2016].

SUNDAY ADELAJA'S BIOGRAPHY

Pastor Sunday Adelaja is the Founder and Senior Pastor of The Embassy of the Blessed Kingdom of God for All Nations Church in Kyiv, Ukraine.

Sunday Adelaja is a Nigerian-born Leader, Thinker, Philosopher, Transformation Strategist, Pastor, Author and Innovator who lives in Kiev, Ukraine.

At 19, he won a scholarship to study in the former Soviet Union. He completed his master's program in Belorussia State University with distinction in journalism.

At 33, he had built the largest evangelical church in Europe — The Embassy of the Blessed Kingdom of God for All Nations.

Sunday Adelaja is one of the few individuals in our world who has been privileged to speak in the United Nations, Israeli Parliament, Japanese Parliament and the United States Senate.

The movement he pioneered has been instrumental in reshaping lives of people in the Ukraine, Russia and about 50 other nations where he has his branches.

His congregation, which consists of ninety-nine percent white Europeans, is a cross-cultural model of the church for the 21st century.

His life mission is to advance the Kingdom of God on earth by raising a generation of history makers who will live for a cause larger, bigger and greater than themselves. Those who will live like Jesus and transform every sphere of the society in every nation as a model of the Kingdom of God on earth.

His economic empowerment program has succeeded in raising over 200 millionaires in the short period of three years.

Sunday Adelaja is the author of over 300 books, many of which are translated into several languages including Russian, English, French, Chinese, German, etc.

His work has been widely reported by world media outlets such as The Washington Post, The Wall Street Journal, New York Times, Forbes, Associated Press, Reuters, CNN, BBC, German, Dutch and French national television stations.

Pastor Sunday is happily married to his "Princess" Bose Dere-Adelaja. They are blessed with three children: Perez, Zoe and Pearl.

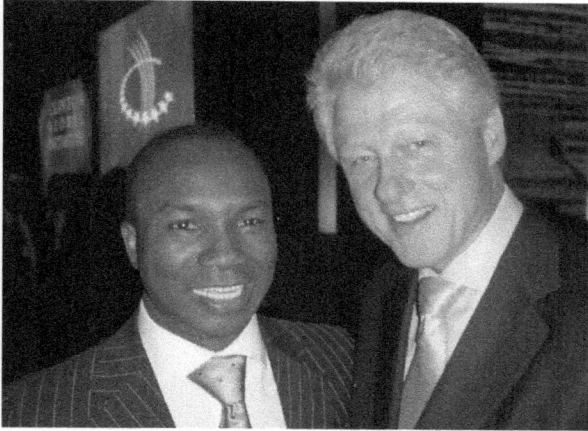

Bill Clinton —
42Nd President Of The
United States (1993–2001),
Former Arcansas State
Governor

Ariel "Arik" Sharon —
Israeli Politician, Israeli
Prime Minister (2001–2006)

Benjamin Netanyahu —
Statesman Of Israel. Israeli
Prime Minister (1996–1999),
Acting Prime Minister
(From 2009)

Jean ChrEtien — Canadian Politician, 20Th Prime Minister Of Canada, Minister Of Justice Of Canada, Head Of Liberan Party Of Canada

Rudolph Giuliani — American Political Actor, Mayor Of New York Served From 1994 To 2001. Actor Of Republican Party

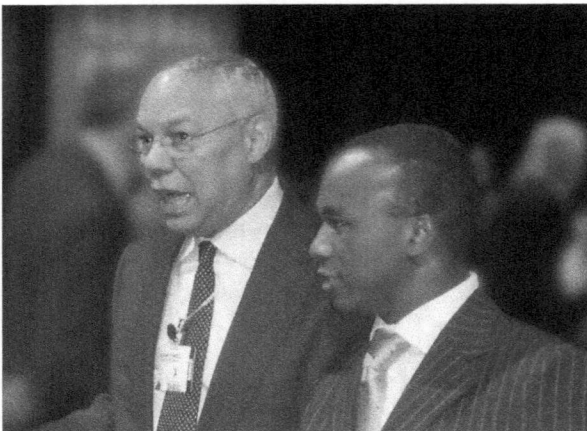

Colin Powell — Is An American Statesman And A Retired Four-Star General In The Us Army, 65Th United States Secretary Of State

Peter J. Daniels —
Is A Well-Known And
Respected Australian
Christian International
Business Statesman Of
Substance

Madeleine
Korbel Albright —
An American Politician And
Diplomat, 64Th United States
Secretary Of State

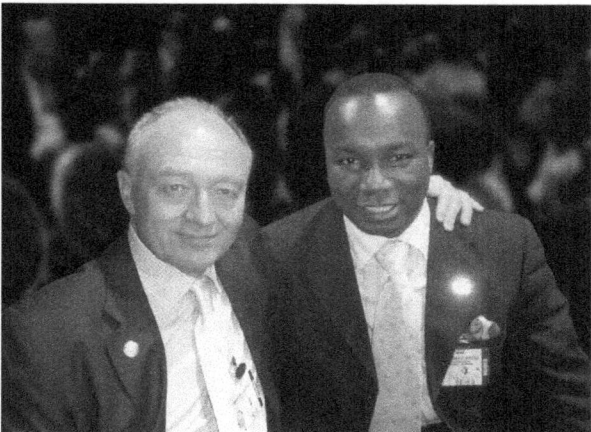

Kenneth Robert
Livingstone —
An English Politician,
1St Mayor Of London
(4 May 2000 – 4 May
2008), Labour Party
Representative

Sir Richard Charles Nicholas Branson —
English Business Magnate, Investor And Philanthropist. He Founded The *Virgin Group*, Which Controls More Than 400 Companies

Mel Gibson —
American Actor And Filmmaker

Chuck Norris —
American Martial Artist, Actor, Film Producer And Screenwriter

Christopher Tucker —
American Actor
And Comedian

Bernice Albertine King —
American Minister Best
Known As The Youngest
Child Of Civil Rights Leaders
Martin Luther King Jr. And
Coretta Scott King Andrew

Andrew Young — American
Politician, Diplomat, And
Activist, 14[Th] United States
Ambassador To The United
Nations, 55[Th] Mayor Of
Atlanta

General Wesley
Kanne Clark —
4-Star General And Nato
Supreme Allied Commander

Dr. Sunday Adelaja's family:
Perez, Pearl, Zoe and Pastor Bose Adelaja

FOLLOW
SUNDAY ADELAJA
ON SOCIAL MEDIA

Subscribe And Read Pastor Sunday's Blog:
www.sundayadelajablog.com
Follow these links and listen to over 200
of Pastor Sunday`s Messages free of charge:
http://sundayadelajablog.com/content/
Follow Pastor Sunday on Twitter:
www.twitter.com/official_pastor

Join Pastor Sunday's Facebook page to stay in touch:
www.facebook.com/pastor.
sunday.adelaja
Visit our websites for more
information about Pastor
Sunday's ministry:
http://www.godembassy.com
http://www.pastorsunday.com
http://sundayadelaja.de

CONTACT

FOR DISTRIBUTION OR TO ORDER
BULK COPIES OF THIS BOOK,
PLEASE CONTACT US:

USA

CORNERSTONE PUBLISHING

info@thecornerstonepublishers.com

+1 (516) 547-4999

www.thecornerstonepublishers.com

AFRICA

SUNDAY ADELAJA MEDIA LTD.

E-mail: btawolana@hotmail.com

+2348187518530, +2348097721451, +2348034093699

LONDON, UK

PASTOR ABRAHAM GREAT

abrahamagreat@gmail.com

+447711399828, +441908538141

KIEV, UKRAINE

pa@godembassy.org

Mobile: +380674401958

BEST SELLING BOOKS BY DR. SUNDAY ADELAJA
AVAILABLE ON AMAZON.COM AND OKADABOOKS.COM

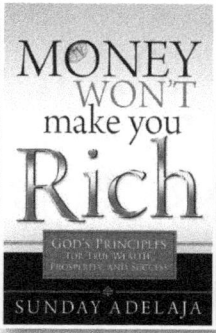

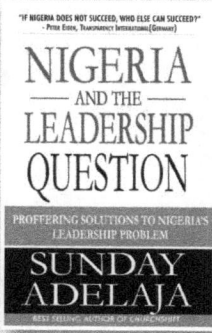

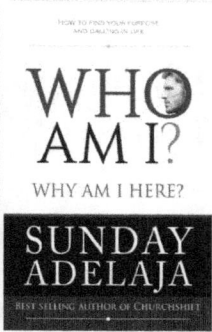

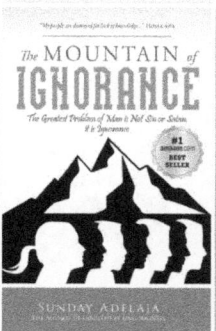

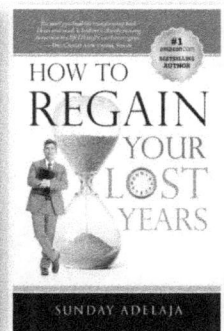

BEST SELLING BOOKS BY DR. SUNDAY ADELAJA
AVAILABLE ON AMAZON.COM AND OKADABOOKS.COM

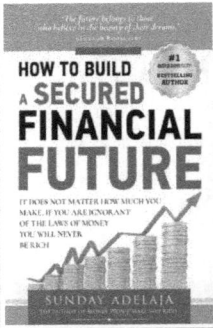

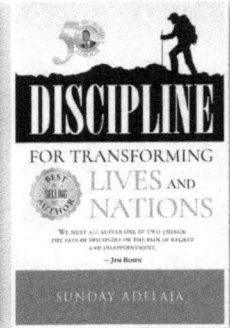

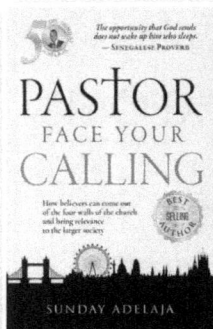

HOW TO BUILD A SECURED FINANCIAL FUTURE — SUNDAY ADELAJA

CREATE YOUR OWN NET WORTH — SUNDAY ADELAJA

RAISING THE NEXT GENERATION OF STEVE JOBS AND BILL GATES — SUNDAY ADELAJA

POVERTY MINDSET VS ABUNDANCE MINDSET — SUNDAY ADELAJA

WHY YOU MUST URGENTLY BECOME A WORKAHOLIC — SUNDAY ADELAJA

HOW TO BECOME GREAT THROUGH TIME CONVERSION — SUNDAY ADELAJA

The NIGERIAN ECONOMY THE WAY FORWARD — SUNDAY ADELAJA

DISCIPLINE FOR TRANSFORMING LIVES AND NATIONS — SUNDAY ADELAJA

PASTOR FACE YOUR CALLING — SUNDAY ADELAJA

WHERE THERE IS PROBLEM THERE IS MONEY — SUNDAY ADELAJA

LIFE IS AN OPPORTUNITY — SUNDAY ADELAJA

BEST SELLING AUTHOR

GOLDEN JUBILEE SERIES BOOKS
BY DR. SUNDAY ADELAJA

FOR DISTRIBUTION OR TO ORDER BULK COPIES OF THIS BOOKS, PLEASE CONTACT US:

USA | CORNERSTONE PUBLISHING
E-mail: info@thecornerstonepublishers.com, +1 (516) 547-4999
www.thecornerstonepublishers.com

AFRICA | SUNDAY ADELAJA MEDIA LTD.
E-mail: btawolana@hotmail.com
+2348187518530, +2348097721451, +2348034093699

LONDON, UK | PASTOR ABRAHAM GREAT
E-mail: abrahamagreat@gmail.com, +447711399828, +441908538141

KIEV, UKRAINE |
E-mail: pa@godembassy.org, Mobile: +380674401958